The Right to Dismiss

The Right to Dismiss

Michael Whincup

COLLINS
8 Grafton Street, London W1

Collins Professional and Technical Books
William Collins Sons & Co. Ltd
8 Grafton Street, London W1X 3LA

First published in Great Britain by
Collins Professional and Technical Books 1986

Distributed in the United States of America
by Sheridan House, Inc.

British Library Cataloguing in Publication Data
Whincup, Michael
The right to dismiss: a handbook for
employers and personnel officers.
1. Employees, Dismissal of—Law and
legislation—Great Britain
I. Title
344.104′12596   KD3110

ISBN 0-00-383244-9

Typeset by V & M Graphics Ltd, Aylesbury, Bucks
Printed and bound in Great Britain by
Mackays of Chatham, Kent

Contents

Preface

We may hope that the days of arbitrary dismissals by ill-tempered foremen and arrogant employers are long since gone, though it is clear we are still paying for the bitter and long-remembered grievances they created. In their place today is an elaborate system of employment protection legislation, developed in turn by Labour and Conservative governments, designed to check abuses, foster individual security and avoid destructive industrial disputes.

Any such system must balance employees' interests in security and stability with employers' needs to respond quickly to changing circumstances or else go under. It must recognise also that while arbitrary dismissal is intolerable, employers have their own interests to protect and must be able to maintain discipline and enforce standards.

No system yet devised can satisfy completely these conflicting demands. The answers given by English law still leave a lot to be desired, particularly, it may be thought, from the employee's point of view. They represent nonetheless a body of rules whose objects are humane and necessary in any civilised society. If studied and understood by both sides of industry they should contribute to a long-term improvement in the climate of industrial relations. If disregarded, they may cost employers dearly.

In the chapters which follow we explain the basic rules as shortly and clearly as possible and give many hundreds of practical examples. Advice is offered also on the conduct of cases at industrial tribunals. The object of this book is to enable management to avoid the many possible pitfalls, but by the same token we hope individual employees and union representatives will find useful guidance on their legal rights.

The Advisory, Conciliation and Arbitration Service Code and consultative document on the revision of the Code are Crown copyright and reproduced by kind permission of the Controller of Her Majesty's Stationery Office.

Michael Whincup
February 1986

Chapter 1

The Contract of Employment

1.01 Introduction

Until a few years ago employers in this country were generally free to sack their employees at any time and for any reason, or for no reason at all but whim or caprice. On his employer's behalf a foreman likewise could give or destroy livelihoods as he pleased. Intimidation, fear and resentment were the natural results, all helping to make British industrial relations what they are today.

The law played little part in all this. It said only that employees were entitled to due notice on dismissal – but since for most people that meant only a week or two, or a few days or even hours, their rights to claim damages for wrongful dismissal if not given their notice were hardly worth having. Where notice is measured in months, however, such a claim may still be valuable, as also where contracts for fixed terms of years and without provision for early termination are ended prematurely.

In post-war days the need for fundamental improvements in security of employment slowly became accepted. The first major change came in 1965 when the Redundancy Payments Act entitled employees dismissed for this one specific reason to lump sum payments from their employers, based on length of service. Payments were intended partly as compensation for loss of employment and partly as protection for the future, and so, it was hoped, would make industrial reorganisation more palatable. Then in 1971 the whole basis of dismissal law was changed by the Conservative government's Industrial Relations Act. The Act introduced the concept of unfair dismissal and required the employer either to justify dismissal or pay compensation, or possibly even re-employ. The standard of fairness involves consideration of each side's interests and the overall merits of their behaviour, and is not determined simply by asking whether or not notice was given. For these purposes, therefore, the question of notice becomes correspondingly unimportant. The 1971 reform was restated in Labour's Trade Union and Labour Relations Act 1974, and now both redundancy and unfair dismissal rules are embodied in the Employment Protection (Consolidation) Act of 1978.

The Employment Protection (Consolidation) Act states various grounds on which dismissal may be proved fair. These are the employee's misconduct, his incapacity, illegality arising from his continued employment, redundancy, or some other substantial reason. If any of these reasons other than redundancy is established then of course the employee has no redress, but if he is dismissed because his work is no longer in demand he is entitled to redundancy pay. The amount of redundancy pay depends on age, length of service and weekly pay. Sums awarded for redundancy are usually less than those given for unfair dismissal. Originally all employers could recover part of their payments from the state, but as from 31 October 1986 only employers with fewer than ten employees are eligible for rebates.

Both unfair dismissal and redundancy claims are decided by industrial tribunals – bodies consisting of a lawyer-chairman and laymen and laywomen, representatives of the TUC and CBI – set up to deal almost exclusively with this kind of work. Industrial tribunals sit in most large towns (see Appendix 1), and are intended to be cheap, speedy and informal in operation. Wrongful dismissal claims, on the other hand, are tried like other breach of contract actions in the county court or High Court, where proceedings are much more formal and delays and costs may be substantial.

1.02 Sources of law

As already indicated, some of our law derives from Act of Parliament, or rules called statutory instruments made under these Acts, and some of it comes from judges' decisions in our higher courts. The judges' decisions are collectively called the common law. Common law deals with issues not directly covered by Parliament, and also with the interpretation of statutes and statutory instruments. The common law has been built up, case by case, over the centuries, and is held together by the doctrine of obligatory precedent.

The doctrine of precedent is a judge-made rule under which statements of legal principle in the highest courts are binding on lower courts in subsequent similar cases. It is important to observe that these statements of principle are often very general in nature and their application depends very largely on the facts of the particular case. Certainly in the context of unfair dismissal and redundancy the vital rules are those laid down by the 1978 Act, not in judgments. The many cases to which we shall refer, particularly those decided by industrial tribunals, are really only examples or illustrations of likely responses in given situations. Precedents in dismissal law are largely cases decided by the Employment Appeal Tribunal or, above that, the Court of Appeal or, ultimately, the House of Lords. The Employment Appeal Tribunal sits also in Glasgow, with appeals to the Court of Session and thence to the House of Lords. The more important tribunal cases and appeals are reported in the Industrial Relations Law Reports, noted in the Table of Cases at the end of the book as I.R.L.R., and appeals are also reported in the Industrial Cases Reports (I.C.R.) or more general series such as the All England Law Reports or Weekly Law Reports (All E.R.: W.L.R.). Certain unreported cases of interest are cited by reference to their tribunal registration numbers. Copies are available from the Central Office of Industrial Tribunals: see [8.01].

The law is divided not only into common law and statute law but also into civil law and criminal law. The role of civil law is broadly to compensate the victim of misfortune or wrongdoing, while criminal law seeks to punish the wrongdoer. For the purposes of this book we confine ourselves almost entirely to the rules of civil law.

1.03 Making the contract

The rest of this chapter discusses issues arising when the contract of employment is made. These questions may seem irrelevant in a book concerned with liability when employment is ended, but they are, in fact, most important. We shall see that there are rules to be observed and steps to be taken at the start of the relationship which may directly affect the outcome of dismissal claims brought perhaps many years later.

1.04   Employee or self-employed?

A surprisingly large number of dismissal cases turn on an issue one might have thought beyond doubt from the start – the question of the worker's status. The 'employer' may argue that the claimant is not in fact his employee and so has no claim under the Employment Protection (Consolidation) Act. The problem arises, of course, because not all workers are employees. Many are self-employed, under contract to provide services for others. The distinction between employee and self-employed or independent contractor is very important in British labour law for many different reasons – not only as regards dismissal but also as it affects tax and insurance, safety, health and welfare rights, union membership rights, maternity pay and reinstatement, and the like. Unfortunately, none of the Acts which create these various rights and duties in employment give any precise guidance as to how the distinction can be drawn. They say only that they apply 'where there is a contract of employment' – and leave it to judges and tribunals to decide whether there is one in the particular case before them.

How, then, can they decide whether a person works under a contract of employment or a contract for services? In both cases there is agreement on one side to do a job and on the other to pay for it. It is not enough just to ask whether the contract is in writing. We shall see that certain basic particulars of contracts of employment are indeed required to be in writing, but if such written provision is made that of itself does not prove the worker is an employee; only that someone thinks he is. And conversely, many independent contractors' contracts are in writing, often in great detail.

One might think that tax and insurance arrangements would provide the answer because, after all, employees are in Schedule E, subject to PAYE, and employers pay insurance contributions on their behalf, while the self-employed are in Schedule D and make their own national insurance payments. But these tests also are inconclusive, since we must ask what lay behind the decision to classify under one Schedule or the other. Such decisions are, in other words, only effects and not causes.

As usual, it is easier to pose the question than to answer it. There is, in fact, no single test or yardstick by which to distinguish between employees and independent contractors. All the elements we have mentioned and many others besides – nature of orders, length of service, frequency and type of payment (whether periodic or lump sum) are relevant, but none is conclusive. As the judge said in one such case: 'Many different tests or criteria have been suggested in many authorities. Any one test may in my view be substantially relevant in one case but largely irrelevant in another' – a 'somewhat negative approach', as he was obliged to admit. It is necessary, in short, to look at the whole relationship, with a view to establishing, very broadly speaking, rights of direction and duties of obedience and accountability on the one hand, or independence, discretion or risk-taking on the other.

In the nineteenth century, the judges said it was all a matter of control – sometimes known as the 'what to do and how to do it' test. The argument was that if one person could tell another what job he must do, and how, when, where and with whom he must do it, then the relationship was necessarily that of employment. But the more these latter details were for the worker to decide, then the more likely was the relationship to be one of principal and independent contractor. With the advent of technology this test became increasingly unrealistic, since many employers could not give detailed instruction because they had far less expertise than their employees – but were nonetheless still their employers. Another suggestion, made by Lord Denning in *Stevenson, Jordan & Harrison* v. *McDonald & Evans* (1952) was that of the integration test. Was the work a vital part of the enterprise, or only incidental to it? If the latter, then again there was a contract for services and not of employment. But this line of inquiry begs as many questions as it answers, and has not proved popular. Other judges have adopted 'common sense' or 'multiple' tests, which unfortunately are so vague as to be almost meaningless.

We can illustrate the difficulties by cases such as *Davis* v. *New*

England College (1977). The college took on a teacher expressly as a 'free-lancer'; the agreement being that he would make his own tax and insurance arrangements. When the job came to an end he sued for compensation for unfair dismissal – on the face of it a blatant attempt to 'have it both ways', to be an independent contractor for some purposes and an employee for others. But which was he? The tribunal looked at the other essential facts of the relationship and found that apart from the tax and insurance arrangements he was treated in all respects like any other teacher-employee, subject to the same degree of supervision, instruction and responsibility. In the circumstances, said the tribunal, he had to be regarded as an employee. The case demonstrates the most important proposition that it is not what the parties call themselves or what they believe to be their relationship that matters, nor what tax or insurance arrangements apply. It is what actually happens between them which determines their relationship. If it were otherwise they could change their status from day to day and make nonsense of the law.

That is not to say that names and taxes and so on are irrelevant. Anyone is free to stop being an employee if he or she wishes, and to set up in business on his or her own account. If the court is satisfied on the evidence that the change in status is a real one, then there can be no claim for compensation for unfair dismissal, as illustrated in *Massey* v. *Crown Life* (1977). A decision as to status for dismissal purposes may require consequential changes in arrangements made for other purposes, notably tax and national insurance, which may possibly be retrospective: *Young* v. *West* (1980).

The position of company directors in particular may sometimes be very uncertain. In law a company is quite separate from its directors, although they may both control and own it. They may therefore be company employees, or act on its behalf as independent contractors, or hold office in it without any contractual relationship. If there is a contract it may be express or implied, but a copy or memorandum of any service agreement must be kept for inspection at the company's registered office. Two contrasting cases on the status of directors are *Parsons* v. *Parsons Ltd* (1979) and *Morley* v. *Morley Ltd* (1985). In *Parsons* the Court of Appeal found a director self-employed because he made his own national insurance contributions, received 'fees and emoluments' and not a salary, and kept no copy of any agreement in the company office (though that fact alone could not determine the outcome). In *Morley* a father and his two sons were the sole directors of a family company. Because of financial difficulties they decided that the father should leave and then that the company should stop trading. All three claimed redundancy pay from the company. Their claims were upheld by the Employment Appeal Tribunal, which accepted first that they were employees of the company because of the terms of their contracts and their full-time commitment to the company, and second that they had been dismissed by it for reasons of redundancy.

Other 'status' cases include *Nethermere* v. *Taverna* (1984), where the Court of Appeal held that an outworker or home worker could be an employee if, as in this case, the contract required the manufacturer to provide work and the home worker to do it, on machinery provided by the manufacturer, despite the fact that the worker could decide for herself on output and hours. But if a manufacturer supplied work only as and when available and the worker could do it or not as he or she thought fit, then evidently there would be a series of contracts for services, not employment. So *Nethermere* does not say all outworkers are employees; only that in certain circumstances they may be. We should note that while the manufacturer's provision of machinery in this case pointed towards a contract of employment, provision of equipment is not itself conclusive.

In *O'Kelly* v. *Trusthouse Forte* (1983), on the other hand, it was held that 'regular casuals', whose services as waiters were frequently sought by Trusthouse Forte and whose work was subject to close supervision, were still independent contractors, largely because there was no obligation on the 'employer' to provide work and no obligation on the workers to accept it. A similar decision was reached in *Hitchcock* v. *Post Office* (1979) where a sub-postmaster was held to be self-employed because of his freedom to delegate work in the office and ability to share in the profits or losses of the business. The more clearly entrepreneurial one's work, in other words, the more clearly one is self-employed. There could be little doubt, for example, that sales representatives travelling in company cars to see company customers in working hours are employees, while insurance salesmen and the like, paid wholly or mainly out of their own endeavours in their own time are likely to be independent contractors.

A related question is the status of agency workers – typists, secretaries, nurses and the like. Depending as much on the facts of the case as on any contract between the parties, they may be employees of the agency (in which case under the Employment Agencies Act 1973 the agency must supply them with written particulars of their employment), or of the hirer – or they may remain self-employed throughout. On the face of it there is no continuing commitment to work or to supply work between worker and agency, and so usually there is no employment relationship. If the agency's purpose is to find people jobs with its clients, those placed should then become the clients' employees, whether they are temporary or permanent. But if the purpose is to provide someone for a specific enterprise or specific period, e.g. a building job, for which he or the agency is paid a lump sum – in effect, a price – then the worker is likely to be an independent contractor. He is the more clearly so if highly skilled and able to decide for himself how and perhaps when to do the job. In that case the hirer can require the agency to withdraw him if he is unsatisfactory, without incurring any liability for so doing. But appearances can be deceptive. Judges and tribunals understand that both parties may say their relationship is that of hirer and contractor in order to avoid employers' liabilities and the burden of income tax. If in reality there are sufficient powers of supervision and control the law will still find a contract of employment: *Graham* v. *Brunswick* (1974). In this case, a 'self-employed' master bricklayer was held to be an employee for the purpose of a site occupier's liability under Factories Act regulations.

Another problem area is that of trainees and apprentices. The courts have said – for example, in *Hawley* v. *Fieldcastle* (1982) – that the relationship of trainer and trainee is not one of employment. This affects, in particular, young people on work experience courses sponsored by the Manpower Services Commission. Yet trainees are now specifically protected against race and sex discrimination as if they were employees and are covered by the Health and Safety at Work Act. In practice the line between training and working may be very difficult to draw, but even so unfair dismissal problems are unlikely to arise because of the two year qualifying period recently introduced: see [3.04].

Apprentices are taken on for both training and working. They are therefore regarded as employees for dismissal purposes, but the teaching and career implications still make the relationship a little different from the ordinary. The courts tend to see employers here as *in loco parentis* – and having responsibilities accordingly – and are inclined to protect apprentices from the consequences of youthful indiscretions. Even so, if the apprentice makes teaching impossible by breaking some basic term of his contract, express or implied, or by failing his examinations, subject to any 'second chance' rules, then he can be dismissed like anyone else. Further reference is made to apprentices under the heading of misconduct: see [5.07].

We stress, then, that there is no easy answer to this first, essential inquiry as to whether a particular worker is an employee or an independent contractor. But once we know he or she is an employee, we still have to find whether he or she is what might very loosely be called a full-timer or a part-timer. Certain statutory rights, notably entitlement to written terms of employment, minimum periods of notice, maternity rights, guarantee or lay-off pay rights and, above all, protection against unfair dismissal and redundancy, are available only to those who have worked for the requisite periods under contracts normally requiring more than sixteen hours' work a week, or who have worked for more than five years under contracts requiring at least eight hours' work a week. This rule is laid down in Schedule 13 of the 1978 Act. The question is always what the contract requires, not what work was actually done in a given week. Average hours are immaterial, unless the contract itself does not specify hours. But a contract requiring more than sixteen hours a week may be reduced to one for eight or more hours for up to twenty-six weeks without affecting continuity of employment. Even with 'sixteen-hour' or full-time workers there are qualifying periods to be served before the various statutory rights apply, as we shall see.

1.05 Written particulars

The next question is whether contracts of employment have to be in writing. The overall answer is 'no'. As a general rule, English law attaches no special significance to writing. We all make contracts every day for which there is never any written evidence – buying a newspaper or cigarettes or petrol, for example – but the agreements are nonetheless binding. But common sense tells us that if the transaction is a complicated one it *ought* to be in writing so as to resolve doubts and make it less a matter of one person's word against another. For these reasons writing is the norm in commercial contracts. And then there are certain exceptional situations where the law sees the transaction as sufficiently complex and far-reaching that it must be in writing – as with insurance, hire purchase and land transactions. So in employment there are exceptions to the general rule and certain particulars have to be in writing. Some of the rules are very old, such as the requirement that contracts of apprenticeship be in writing; others, more important for us here, are of recent origin.

The most important rules were introduced in the Contracts of Employment Act of 1963 and are now to be found in sections 1 and 2 of the Employment Protection (Consolidation) Act 1978. With exceptions noted immediately below, they apply to employees working over sixteen hours a week and to those who have worked more than eight hours a week for five years. They provide that within thirteen weeks of starting work (or after the five years have elapsed, as the case may be) employees must receive written statements of certain basic particulars of their employment. The personal details must appear in the statement itself; other provisions which are the same for other employees may be given by reference to some conveniently accessible 'central' document such as a copy of the collective agreement in the works office.

The statement must record the names of the employer and employee; the date employment began; whether any previous employment counts towards continuity of employment, and if so when the period of continuous employment began; the date the contract ends if it is for a fixed term, and the job title. It must also tell the employee whom to see if dissatisfied with a disciplinary decision or in order to pursue a grievance at work. The following further information required by the Act is usually given by reference to a copy of the collective agreement: pay; hours; holidays and holiday pay (in detail sufficient to enable the employee to calculate his or her own entitlement); sickness and sick pay arrangements; disciplinary rules and grievance procedures other than those concerning safety and health at work; notice and pension rights.

Employees who need not be given these written statements are those in Crown service, including National Health Service employees, people normally working abroad, and those whose written contracts already contain the various particulars. In practice, the Crown makes the same provision for its employees as is required by the Act.

Several points arising from these rules bear more or less directly on dismissal rights. We should note first that the main purpose of the written statement is only to record that which has already been agreed, which may have been by word of mouth at the interview or perhaps, in some respects, even taken for granted. There is accordingly no need to vary or add to the existing agreement to comply with the Act. If, for example, the company has no private sick pay scheme it is only necessary to record that the state scheme applies. It follows that the statement should not be regarded as 'the contract': it is only written evidence of some of its terms. Many other terms such as place of work – which may be expressly recorded or may have to be deduced from such diverse sources as the original advertisement for the job, things said at interview or in letters of acceptance, the collective agreement, works rules books and even custom and practice – must also be taken into account, and common sense suggests that all important details of this kind should be in writing.

Once the various prescribed particulars are duly recorded then of course each side should know where it stands on these matters. If there are omissions or disputes as to meaning, either side may seek a ruling from an industrial tribunal. Such ruling will be based on other available evidence, e.g. the collective agreement or custom and practice within the industry. An employee may still dispute the written statement even though he has signed it, since signature may prove only receipt of the statement and not necessarily agreement with it. Apart from the possibility of an industrial tribunal declaration there is no direct method of enforcing the written statement rule, and some employers therefore disregard it. The inevitable result is to leave in doubt matters which ought to be certain, and if that in turn leads to disputes and thence to dismissal the employer may well be to blame because it was his own initial failure which began the sequence of events.

Two particular items in the written statement need to be looked at in more detail – the reference to employment with another employer, and the job title. As regards the first point, protection against unfair dismissal and redundancy depends, as we see in later chapters, on length of service, and in certain limited circumstances service with a previous employer may be counted. These circumstances are set out at length in Chapter 7 in the context of redundancy rights.

1.06   Job descriptions

The other matter of more immediate interest in the written statement is the job title. A person's job title is clearly of the utmost importance in determining his or her status and rate of pay, but can scarcely explain the nature of the job in detail. That becomes a major issue when the employee disobeys an order on the grounds that it is not his job, and the confrontation leads as it so often does to dismissal. Disputes of this kind can be avoided, or at least their frequency can be very much reduced, by the provision of written job descriptions to supplement the job title. We have seen that the law does not demand written job descriptions, but to provide them at the outset of employment is one of the most useful things an employer can do in order to avoid liability at the end. Indeed, in view of the countless dismissal cases which turn on delineation of duties, it is difficult to overstate the importance of so doing.

Employers might well say that to give every employee a written job description would take a great deal of unnecessary time and effort, and might also be self-defeating in the sense that the more a job is discussed and defined the more scope there is for demarcation disputes. Employees themselves and their representatives may be equally disinclined to have their duties recorded in order to allow themselves more latitude and room for argument. The objections are considerable, but the advantages for both sides seem clearly to outweigh them.

Drafting a job description is in itself a skilled occupation, and methods and opinions differ as to how it may best be done. Some employers seek to cover every contingency and produce documents several pages long. The weakness of this approach is its thoroughness. If the employer seems to be trying to list every aspect of the job, then when the employee is asked to do something which is not listed he or she has every reason to refuse. In any case it is not possible to write down everything a person may be required to do over a period of years, and the attempt to do so may preclude natural or necessary developments in the job – a theme to which we return shortly.

Preferably, then, and so far as circumstances permit, the employer might try to confine himself to just two or three sentences or short paragraphs to supplement the job title. The first sentence or paragraph would then contain the four or five key words or phrases which are of the essence of the job; which describe, in other words, the general nature of the daily duties. The second sentence or paragraph should provide for any mobility or transferability requirements the employer might have in mind. Many cases have turned on this particular issue. The employer may well have agreed on transferability terms with the union, but it turns out often enough that he has never mentioned them to the employee, and so naturally when he tries to enforce the agreement there is trouble. Thirdly, the statement should contain what might be called an *et cetera* clause – a clause whose effect is to require the employee to do anything reasonably incidental to the duties specified above.

Et cetera clauses may, of course, lead to suspicion and objection among employees because of their apparent uncertainty. They are nonetheless, at least in the present author's opinion, both necessary and desirable. An example of their use is in *Briggs* v. *I.C.I.* (1968). Mr Briggs was a process worker at I.C.I. in Billingham. His contract said, among other things: 'You must accept the right of management to transfer you to another job on higher or lower rates of pay, whether day work, night work or shift work'. On its face, such wording entitled I.C.I. to move him from one plant to another at the other end of the country, or, if it were argued that he was confined to Billingham, then up and down through the ranks from worker-director to floor-sweeper and back again as they pleased. How, then, should the clause be interpreted? On Mr Briggs' claim for redundancy pay the industrial tribunal held that I.C.I. was entitled only to move him from one process worker's job at

Billingham to another process worker's job at Billingham. The very limited scope thus given to words of apparently almost limitless effect was reached by reference to his job title and the specified place of work. That in turn tells us that these general clauses are interpreted in the light of what is particularised, and their effect thus very much reduced. Despite such very wide wording, one might say, management 'can't get away with murder'.

On the other hand, such clauses are intended to give and do in fact give management some room to manoeuvre, which is very much in management's interest. It could be said that they are therefore also in the worker's interest, in the sense that if management has no room to manoeuvre, i.e. to adapt to change, then the enterprise is dead and so the worker loses his livelihood. But that may not be a very popular line of argument.

A further reflection on *et cetera* clauses is that they are sometimes left out of employees' contracts because of union resistance – yet in practice omission achieves less than nothing. There is no doubt at law that employees have got to do whatever is reasonably incidental to their specified duties, whether or not the contract expressly says so. It is in everybody's interest, therefore, to write that down before –hand and have it plainly understood from the start.

But what *is* reasonably incidental to a man's day's work? That is another question altogether, the answer to which depends very largely on the nature of his job. Examples are given among our cases on dismissal for incapacity and misconduct (see Chapters 4 and 5) but one might by way of simple illustration suggest that most if not all employees would be obliged to help out on a short-term basis to cover absent colleagues who do the same kind of work. That may well be unobjectionable when applied to colleagues absent through illness, but there seems no logical reason why it should not apply also to colleagues absent on strike – though that conclusion might be somewhat less generally acceptable. The fact remains that the employee is on the premises solely because of his contract of employment and his primary loyalty in that connection is to his employer and not to his fellow employees. A specific illustration, which involved suspension rather than dismissal but could have led to dismissal, is *Gorse* v. *Durham County Council* (1971), where supervision of school meals was held reasonably incidental to current teaching duties.

These issues have arisen in connection with the written statement of terms of employment. Two remaining aspects should be briefly mentioned. It will be recalled first that the written statement must refer to the employer's grievance and disciplinary procedure, which should itself be in writing and preferably issued in full to each employee. In Chapter 6 we consider more fully the drafting of such procedures and the consequences for the employer of failure to follow his own rules. Finally, we should note what the Act says about changing the terms recorded in the written statement. It is clear that changes of some sort must take place sooner or later, if only in rates of pay. We pursue below and in Chapter 5 the permissible extent of such changes. Assuming here, however, that the changes are acceptable, section 4 of the 1978 Act requires only that they be stated in writing within one month after they take effect, or, if the terms were originally given by reference to the collective agreement, should be noted up in the collective agreement, again within one month. Changes in the employer's name but not identity need not be notified, nor changes in identity which do not affect continuity of employment (as to which, see Chapter 7).

1.07 The terms of employment

We turn now to consider the contents of the contract of employment. Within limits, employer and employee are free to agree on whatever terms and conditions they wish, by individual or collective bargaining. Once the terms are agreed upon, the contract is binding and either side can sue or be sued for breach of contract. If it is the employee who is in breach he may face the additional or alternative penalty of dismissal, which in practice is far and away the most common remedy.

1.08 Collective agreements

Although many terms in individuals' contracts are agreed collectively, i.e. between management and union, the collective agreement is fundamentally different from the individual's contract in that it is not in itself legally enforceable. Section 18 of the Labour Government's Trade Union and Labour Relations Act 1974, still in force, says that collective agreements are of no legal significance unless they state in writing that they are to be enforceable – a most unlikely event. It will be seen that this is a crucial statement of Labour philosophy with regard to legal intervention in union affairs, and one which, we may observe, distinguishes Britain from almost every other industrial country. The law thus regards collective agreements as 'gentlemen's agreements' or 'binding in honour only' – an example, perhaps, of the legendary British sense of humour. That is not to say, however, that such agreements are entirely devoid of legal effect. If, as is commonly the case, the individual's contract incorporates the terms of a collective agreement then those terms become enforceable by and against that individual.

Collective agreements may be incorporated in individuals' contracts either by statutory provision, as in teaching and the Health Service, or by some express statement to that effect in the contract, e.g. that as regards pay, hours, etc., 'your terms and conditions are in accordance with the current agreement between the company and your union'. In *N.C.B* v. *Galley* (1958) the collective agreement incorporated in each individual's contract provided for work on 'such days or parts of days as may reasonably be required by management'. Employees who refused to work Saturday shifts were therefore held liable for the cost of replacement labour. The same result may be achieved without express incorporation but by long-standing observance of collective agreements on both sides – *Mordecai* v. *Beatus* (1975) – or where the union negotiates the terms as agent for its members (which is not the usual relationship).

Difficulties may still arise in deciding *which* terms of a collective agreement are incorporated, whether incorporation is express or implied. Many terms are essentially collective and incapable of application to individuals. In *B.L.* v. *McQuilken* (1978), for example, management agreed with the union to advise and assist certain employees faced with redundancy. This particular employee complained of the difficulties he faced because he had not been advised and assisted in accordance with the agreement, and so resigned and sued for compensation for unfair dismissal. His claim was rejected because the agreement was viewed as a statement of managerial policy *vis-à-vis* the union and not a right vested thereupon in each employee and capable of enforcement by him. It has been held also that since collective agreements are unenforceable, the ending of such an agreement has no effect upon individual contracts based upon it: *Gibbons* v. *A.B.P.* (1985).

Another possible source of obligation is custom and practice at the place of work, or within the industry. A custom will be upheld if it is reasonably certain, known to both parties and consistent with terms expressly agreed. In *Sagar* v. *Ridehalgh* (1930) a wage deduction for bad workmanship was held to be in accordance with a trade custom which the employee was deemed to have accepted when he began work. In *Bird* v. *British Celanese* (1945) there was a similar ruling on the right to suspend without pay – which would otherwise have been in breach of contract – in that particular job. Where ambulance men customarily took urgent calls at any time, a man who refused a call because it would interfere with his lunch was held properly dismissed: *Smith* v. *St. Andrews Ambulance Service* (1973).

1.09   Rights and duties added by law

The gross imbalance in bargaining power which characterised management-labour relations in the past, which still persists in some areas today, and for which it seems we must all still continue to pay, has led in this century to many attempts by law to curb exploitation and abuse. In a book on dismissal we cannot describe all these laws in detail, but must take due note that they exist and that they represent variously minimum standards of employment below which no-one may fall and boundaries within which collective or individual bargaining must take place. It will be appreciated also that breach of these legal requirements may become a cause of dispute and so possibly of dismissal.

In particular, we should mention the mass of civil and criminal safety obligations on employers (and note dismissal issues arising from them in Chapter 5); the minimum wage levels set by wages councils for over two million workers in under-unionised and notoriously underpaid industries such as catering, agriculture and outwork; the rules against discrimination on grounds of sex, race, union membership and spent convictions (which as they affect dismissals are detailed in Chapter 3); rights to equal pay for equal work; maternity pay and reinstatement rights; rights of officials of recognised unions to reasonable time off with pay (the time off being a matter for agreement rather than unilateral action) for industrial relations work and training; rights to time off for public duties; rights of members of recognised unions to reasonable time off to take part in union activities (which exclude strike action); duties upon employers to give recognised unions information needed for collective bargaining, and so on – all quite apart from the rules about notice, dismissal and redundancy which are our primary concern. All these statutory provisions are supplemented by common law requirements as to good faith and the like which serve as implied terms of contracts of employment, and breach of which may justify dismissal. We enlarge upon these implied terms in Chapter 2.

1.10   Changing the terms

Subject to this 'floor' of legal rights and duties and the law of the land in general, employer and employee can agree on whatever terms they please. But having once made their agreement, how far are they free to change it? If they agree to change, there is no problem. The difficulties arise when the employer seeks to compel acceptance of new terms and conditions, a situation equivalent to strike action in support of new demands by employees. Both sides must recognise that the contract of employment necessarily represents a continuing relationship – not a once-for-all transaction as in a contract of sale in a shop. Up to a point, therefore, it must be expected to change and develop. Both sides must be prepared to adapt themselves to changing circumstances – though in practice the pressures are often more clearly upon employees.

It is difficult if not impossible to say how far we can extend this idea of inherent flexibility in employment contracts. But we could certainly argue that it extends, again within reason, to the way a job is done and the circumstances in which it is done. The issue in

Cresswell v. *Inland Revenue* (1984), for example, was whether tax assessors could be obliged under their contracts to work with computers and visual display units, which they said involved new skills and affected job satisfaction and for which they demanded additional pay. The judge rejected their claim:

'There can really be no doubt that an employee is expected to adapt himself to new methods and new techniques introduced in the course of his employment ... In an age when the computer has forced its way into the schoolroom, and where electronic games are played by schoolchildren in their own homes as a matter of everyday occurrence, it can hardly be considered that to ask an employee to acquire basic skills as to retrieving information from a computer, or feeding such information into a computer, is something in the slightest esoteric, or even, nowadays, unusual.'

It follows that if this had been a dismissal case and not a pay claim the employee would have lost on the same ground.

A somewhat similar case was *Royle* v. *Trafford B.C.* (1984) where a teacher of a class of thirty-two refused to take four more children into his class as required by the employer. The class size was held to be a matter for the employer's discretion – subject of course to some practical limit which only a judge could determine on the facts and figures put before him.

Somehow a distinction must be drawn between these permissible and, indeed, inevitable areas of change on the one hand and imposition of more fundamental changes on the other. On the face of it, a new place of work – in the sense of new premises on a different site – or reduced rates of pay or alterations in job content are all more vital issues, and so employers' attempts to compel acceptance, perhaps by threatening dismissal, may well be seen as breaches of contract. But even here we cannot guarantee the outcome. Some of the unfair dismissal cases discussed in Chapters 3 and 5, where this issue is pursued at greater length, show that employers may escape liability even for changes such as these if they can prove that their demands upon their employees are necessary responses to new business pressures.

We must remember also that many employees' contracts contain the kind of mobility or transferability clauses mentioned earlier in this chapter. If a contract expressly provides for transfer from one end of the country to the other the employee must go when he is told, however long he might have been in the one place and however well he might have settled there. And if his contract expressly allows for a variable job content, again he must accept such variations.

Even if the contract does not expressly provide for mobility, the judge or tribunal may regard it as inherent in the work in question – for example, in building work, and perhaps more generally at managerial level. For most employees, however, there is no implied duty to move wherever required within the employer's area of operations. So in *O'Brien* v. *Associated Fire Alarms* (1969) the Court of Appeal held that men who lived and worked in Liverpool could fairly be expected to work anywhere in the Liverpool area, but in the absence of express contractual commitment were not obliged to go to Barrow-in-Furness merely because the employer was in business there also.

We have tried in this chapter to define what we mean by 'employee', and to explain the importance of a decision on that fundamental point. We have considered how far a contract of employment is required to be in writing, and then to explain its relation to the collective agreement. Finally, we have discussed at some length the contents of the contract, express and implied. With all these preliminaries in mind we can move on to ways of ending the contract and incurring or avoiding liability accordingly.

Chapter 2

Wrongful Dismissal

2.01 Breach of contract

An employer may be liable for dismissal under one or more of three main headings – wrongful dismissal, unfair dismissal or redundancy. In this chapter we discuss the rules of wrongful dismissal, noting as we go along how they differ from those on unfair dismissal which make up the bulk of this book.

Wrongful dismissal, unlike unfair dismissal, always involves a breach of contract by the employer. Either he has dismissed summarily when under the contract he should have given notice, or he has ended before time a contract for a fixed term and with no provision for earlier termination, or he has ended without good cause a contract whose terms expressly or by implication require him to show cause. Contracts of this latter kind are usually found in higher management circles or among public office-holders (such as chairmen of health authorities and chief constables), but also include apprenticeships. We might note in passing that appointment expressly for a probationary period does not of itself preclude dismissal within that period – *Dalgleish* v. *Kew House* (1982) – nor does appointment to a 'permanent post', or other such wording, necessarily guarantee a lifetime's security. Wording of this kind may mean no more than 'pensionable' or 'full-time', as was held in *Clarke* v. *I.B.C.* (1974), a New Zealand case.

2.02 Damages

Breach of contract is a common law wrong whose remedy is almost always a claim for damages. Claims for up to £5000 are heard in the county court and for sums above that in the High Court, or in Scotland the Sheriff Court. They cannot be decided by industrial tribunals, which by statute can only hear unfair dismissal and redundancy claims. People employed in public offices under statutory provisions may apply to the High Court for judicial review of the propriety of their dismissal, as in *R* v. *Secretary of State, ex parte Benwell* (1985), where the Court quashed a dismissal reached in breach of the Prison Rules. But private contractual rights cannot be enforced that way: *R* v. *East Berkshire H.A., ex parte Walsh* (1984). Breach of contract claims must be begun within six years of the alleged breach, whereas in unfair dismissals the limit is three months.

Damages are to compensate for loss, and essentially the only loss the law recognises in wrongful dismissal is that of money due during the proper period of notice or unexpired period of the contract, as the case may be, plus loss of fringe benefits – use of car, etc. – during that time. Entitlement to notice might, however, be extended in accordance with the time limits of any rights of appeal given by the contract: *Gunton* v. *Richmond L.B.C.* (1980). Damages might be increased by a small amount to cover loss of protection against unfair dismissal – *Stapp* v. *Shaftesbury Society* (1982) – as also where the contract was intended to provide benefits additional to salary, such as an actor's opportunities for publicity or, in the case of a wrongfully ended apprenticeship, loss of training and prospects: *Dunk* v. *Waller* (1970). Bonus or other entirely discretionary payments cannot be claimed: *Lavarack* v. *Woods* (1966). There is no claim for humiliation or distress arising out of the circumstances of dismissal, as held by the House of Lords in *Addis* v. *Gramophone Co.* (1909), and recently re-affirmed in *Shove* v. *Downs* (1984). If defamation is alleged in the circumstances of dismissal, that is, of course, a separate legal issue.

Compensation in unfair dismissal cases, on the other hand, is assessed on a quite different basis – that of overall economic loss, under statutory principles and within statutory limits, as described in Chapter 9. One notable aspect of the distinction between common law and statutory claims is that only in wrongful dismissal cases can information about the employee which does not come to light until after the dismissal be used to justify it: *Boston* v. *Ansell* (1888). In unfair dismissal such after-acquired information cannot make fair a dismissal which would otherwise be unfair, but may have the effect of reducing the amount of compensation payable: *Devis* v. *Atkins* (1977).

It will be seen that for anyone employed under a short period of notice a claim for wrongful dismissal is hardly worth bringing. Almost certainly a claim for compensation for unfair dismissal would be more lucrative, assuming the employee has served the necessary qualifying period (see Chapter 3). And even where more substantial sums of money are at stake, the employee is unlikely to recover all his losses because he has a duty to try to reduce them. The common law rules on 'mitigation of loss' (which apply equally in unfair dismissal cases) oblige him to seek employment elsewhere as soon as he can or possibly even to accept some less agreeable alternative post offered by his former employer. But he need not take substantially different work, nor necessarily 'up sticks' in search of it. These points are illustrated in *Yetton* v. *Eastwoods Froy* (1966). The case concerned a managing director on £7500 a year who, after a take-over, was demoted to assistant manager at the same rate of pay. This was a clear breach of contract and serious loss of status at a vital point in his career. He left and tried but failed to find employment at the same level elsewhere. Eventually he applied for jobs offering around £4000 p.a. but refused to apply for one at £2500. The High Court held that he was not obliged to accept such demotion and that he had made every reasonable effort to find other work. He was awarded substantial damages for losses suffered up to the time of trial, but not a great deal for future loss because the judge still thought he would soon find other suitable employment.

Damages for wrongful dismissal are further reduced by the amount of tax the dismissed employee would have paid on earnings during the proper period of notice. In the altogether exceptional case where damages of more than £25,000 are awarded, the plaintiff himself must pay tax on any amount over that figure. Deductions are made also for unemployment pay received and social security contributions saved.

2.03 Employers' defences

But how can the employer avoid liability in the first place? He can only do this by proving a breach of contract by the employee sufficient to excuse his own apparent breach in dismissing him without notice. Some substantial form of wrongdoing by the employee, deliberate or otherwise, must therefore be established – a clear disregard of an important term of the contract, or breach of contractual duty implied by the common law. These implied terms represent what the courts see as necessary norms of behaviour on both sides, though they weigh particularly on employees. The obligations involved here are those of good faith, obedience, competence and care.

2.04 Good faith

The employee's duty to act in good faith requires him to do his job with honesty and integrity and not to allow conflicts of interest to arise beyond those inherent in the management-labour relationship. The duty is usually expressed in negative terms – not to steal, not to sell trade secrets, not to compete, and so on. There is no positive obligation to do a fair day's work for a fair day's pay – perhaps because of the difficulty of defining either of these elements – but certainly employees must not act in such a way as to defeat the purpose of employment – for example, by working to rule in order to bring the job to a standstill: *Secretary of State* v. *A.S.L.E.F.* (1972). In certain limited circumstances there may be a duty to cooperate beyond the letter of one's contract, such as in health service or other 'life or death' cases. Several cases suggest also an obligation to accept changes in hours and other such terms and conditions brought about by business necessity. Examples are given in Chapters 3 and 5.

The scope and effect of the good faith rule is shown in more detail by cases such as *Sinclair* v. *Neighbour* (1966). A betting shop manager who knew his employer would not let him take money from the till nonetheless borrowed £15 without permission, though without dishonest intent. He left a signed IOU and replaced the money the next day. On discovering what he had done his employer dismissed him. The court upheld his dismissal since although the employer was not out of pocket the manager had shown himself a bad risk, willing to break a basic term of his employment. 'It was incumbent upon him as manager to keep the till inviolate', said the judge. (But it does not follow that every 'loan', however small and well-intentioned, always justifies dismissal. In *How* v. *Tesco* (1974) employees working on tills were forbidden to carry their own money or to take money from the tills, but in a 'whip round' for the manager's new baby an operator took 50p from the till and forgot to make it up. The dismissal was held to be unfair.)

Employees must look after customers' and clients' interests on the firm's behalf and not their own. They must not, for example, arrange to take on clients' business for their own purposes. In *Normalec* v. *Britton* (1983), the employee used confidential information about his employer's customers in setting up his own business. This was held to entitle his employer to all the profits of that business. Similarly, in the Canadian case of *Protective Plastics* v. *Hawkins* (1964), an employee had within the four months before he left work arranged to join a competitor, collected confidential information from his employer, told customers he was leaving and generally neglected his work. The employer was held entitled to recover one third of the salary paid during that time.

It is widely believed that what an employee does in his own time is his own business, but that is not necessarily so. Working for a competitor in one's spare time will be seen as bad faith if a real conflict of interest or harmful effect upon working capacity can be shown. The remedies here may include an injunction as well as damages and/or dismissal. Illustrations of successful actions by employers include *Hivac* v. *Park Royal Scientific Instruments* (1946) where skilled manual workers were employed on Sundays by a rival company in a highly specialised field, and *Bartlett* v. *Shoe and Leather Record* (1960) where an editor was held in breach of faith by making numerous well-paid contributions to other publications on topics covered by his own trade journal.

Many other out of hours activities may be equally harmful to the employer, directly or indirectly. Violent or dishonest behaviour away from work is as likely to suggest unfitness for office or to damage the employer's reputation as if it took place at work. The same may be true of conduct which while lawful is still regarded as immoral or otherwise socially unacceptable. It is not a question of the employer's approval or disapproval, but of whether the conduct is detrimental to his business, e.g. because of the reactions of other employees or the public. Changes in public standards must be borne in mind when considering the cases. In *Clouston* v. *Corry* (1906) a manager was held properly dismissed after a conviction for drunk and disorderly behaviour in a hotel and for using obscene language in the presence of women. A married professor's dismissal for seducing a female student was upheld in *Orr* v. *University of Tasmania* (1957). But dismissal of a manager accused by his employer of being 'a great pincher of bottoms and breasts' was not justified when he was found only to have touched two women on the bottom on isolated occasions and to have used bad language. He was awarded substantial damages accordingly: *Myers* v. *Mono* (1970). An employee who is a heavy gambler may be a bad risk if he works in a position of trust: *Pearce* v. *Foster* (1885).

The same general considerations apply even to a worker's private beliefs – for example, if he is employed in government service. The House of Lords accepted in *R* v. *Secretary of State ex parte Council of Civil Service Unions* (1985) that in the interests of national security an employee might be obliged to give up union membership or face dismissal. In the New Zealand case of *Deynzer* v. *Campbell* (1950) the position was explained as follows:

> 'A servant owes a duty of loyalty to his employer's interests and if he develops opinions or associations, whether political or otherwise, which do or might endanger the interests of his employer then he cannot complain if his employer takes steps by way of dismissal or transfer to other work so as to abate the danger, [especially where] the department in which the plaintiff was employed is one in which the loyalty and discretion of its components cannot be in doubt.'

An employee also risks dismissal if he does not pass on to management any information he may have of material dishonesty among fellow employees, more particularly if he himself is in a responsible position. But does good faith require an employee to report his own shortcomings? The usual and more realistic answer is 'no', but there are exceptions to every rule. In *Sybron* v. *Rochem* (1983) a director was held rightly dismissed because he did not tell his company of a conspiracy among fellow employees to set themselves up in competition – albeit he only knew of the conspiracy because he was a party to it, and was thus bound to incriminate himself.

As regards an applicant's suitability for employment, it is for the employer to ask the questions rather than for the applicant to volunteer information which may harm his prospects – unless his silence amounts to fraud. If the question is asked and a deliberately false answer given then bad faith is established. But dismissal may still not be justified if the matter is trivial or the employee's merits proved by subsequent good service. These general principles are subject to the provisions of the Rehabilitation of Offenders Act 1974, as noted in Chapter 3.

2.05 Employers' good faith

The rules of good faith cut both ways. Employers must not behave arbitrarily or unreasonably, or so as to destroy the necessary basis of mutual confidence. In *Cox* v. *Phillips* (1975), for example, an employee who was demoted in breach of contract and who then felt obliged to resign successfully claimed damages for wrongful dismissal. He was also awarded compensation for the distress and depression suffered because of the breach of contract (which, curiously enough, he could not have recovered if he had sued only for wrongful dismissal: see [2.02]).

In *Bliss* v. *S.E. Thames Regional Health Authority* (1985) the Authority ordered a consultant to submit to a psychiatric examination and suspended him when he refused to do so. It was an implied term of the contract that the Authority *could* require him to undergo a medical examination, but only if they had reasonable grounds for believing he might be suffering from a disability which could harm his patients. Here the Authority could prove only a severe breakdown in relationships between the consultant and his colleagues. The requirement and the penalty therefore amounted to a fundamental breach of the Authority's duty not to act in a way likely to damage or destroy the relationship of trust and confidence necessary between employer and employee, and the Authority was held liable for wrongful dismissal.

While the normal remedy for breach of contract is damages, there are also some very limited circumstances in which an aggrieved employee might seek the alternative of an injunction. In *Irani* v. *Southampton H.A.* (1985) a consultant was given six weeks' notice in accordance with his contract, but without regard to dismissal procedures laid down in Whitley Council terms and conditions. He succeeded in his High Court claim for an injunction to prevent dismissal until the procedures had been followed.

When we come to look at unfair dismissal we shall see that these same issues of reciprocal good faith arise also in the context of constructive dismissal.

2.06 Competence and care

Looking now at the remaining common law duties of competence, care and obedience, we should mention in particular the instructive case of *Superlux* v. *Plaisted* (1958). A vacuum cleaner salesman arrived home late at night with his van still full of vacuum cleaners. Since he had no garage he had to decide whether to carry them all into his house or leave them in the locked van under a street light. He left them there locked, but overnight they were stolen. The employer sued him for damages for breach of his implied duty to do his job carefully – a remedy additional or alternative to dismissal. The judge said that the standard of care employees had to observe in relation to their employers' goods and interests was at least as high as if they were their own – a very high standard indeed. It was reasonably clear that the employee would not have found it too much trouble to take his own goods into the house, which was much the safer course, or, putting it another way, that he would have had only himself to blame if he had left his own goods exposed and unguarded all night and they had been stolen. He was therefore held liable for the value of the lost vacuum cleaners. Similar cases have imposed liability for thefts from unguarded or unlocked vehicles: *Marshall* v. *Sloan* (1981).

We stress that the employer always needs to show some significant loss or damage, actual or likely, before he can sue or dismiss. This burden was easily discharged in *Janata Bank* v. *Ahmed* (1981), where a bank manager was held liable in damages for omitting to make proper inquiries about his customers' credit-worthiness, as a result of which the bank was defrauded of large sums of money. If the loss is serious it does not matter whether it was caused accidentally or deliberately, nor in a single major incident or several minor ones.

If the employer's loss is caused partly by his own fault, for example by failure to give appropriate instructions, any compensation he claims will be reduced accordingly. On the other hand, the employer's failure in the *Superlux* case above to ask his salesman whether he had garage or storage space, when in fact he had neither, could not relieve the employee of his continuing duty to look after the goods in his possession to the best of his ability.

2.07   Obedience

As regards obedience, the position is that wilful refusal of a lawful and reasonable order must be a breach of contract, and likely as such to result in dismissal and/or damages. The requirement of wilfulness tells us that disobedience resulting from misunderstanding or inadvertence – or a conflict of loyalties between different supervisors as in *Laws* v. *London Chronicle* (1959) – is insufficient. Merely to query orders or complain about working conditions is not disobedience. Refusal may be by words or conduct – for example, by walking out or working to rule – if the object is to stop the enterprise in its tracks: *Secretary of State* v. *A.S.L.E.F.* (1972). Abuse or rudeness by an employee may also amount to rejection of the employer's authority, but much depends on the words used, provocation or lack of it, and accepted levels of give and take.

There can be no question of wilful refusal if the employer's orders are not 'lawful and reasonable' in the first place. Lawfulness and reasonableness are determined by the express or implied terms of the contract, which may include the terms of a collective agreement. It will be recalled from Chapter 1 that, in addition to their basic duties, employees must undertake whatever is reasonably incidental to their work, whether or not that obligation is expressly stated. We have also observed that the scope of the employee's duties may be affected by changes introduced by the employer, with or without the employee's agreement. The extent of the employer's powers in this respect is discussed further in Chapters 3 and 5 (see [3.10] and [5.05]).

We should note here, however, that orders involving risk of injury over and above what is normal in the job are not lawful or reasonable and can properly be disobeyed. A pilot dismissed for refusing to fly an unsafe aircraft was awarded damages in *Donovan* v. *Invicta Airlines* (1970). This case also indicated that employers must give their orders with due civility. On the other hand it was held lawful in *Buckoke* v. *G.L.C.* (1971) for employers to instruct firemen to cross traffic lights at red if they thought it safe to do so. Differences of opinion about the safety of a job may ultimately have to be resolved by expert evidence in court. So in *N.C.B.* v. *Hughes* (1959) a group of miners stopped work because they said the coal face was exceptionally dangerous. The Board sued them for damages for breach of contract. On the evidence put before him by both sides, the judge decided that the face was no more dangerous than usual. The men's refusal to work was therefore unjustified, and so each was held liable to compensate the Board for the value of his lost output. Suing one's employees for damages cannot be recommended as a way of fostering good will, but may occasionally be thought useful to establish a point of principle or, of course, to recover a large sum of money.

Wrongful dismissal, then, is by no means a dead letter either in law or practice. Many of the issues raised are fundamental to the employment relationship, and by no means all of them can be resolved by reference to recent employment protection legislation. From day to day, however, the problem more likely to confront employers who have taken or wish to take disciplinary action is that of liability for unfair dismissal, to which topic we now turn.

Chapter 3

Unfair Dismissal – and How to Avoid It

3.01 The need for reform

We have seen that, in the past, employers seeking to dismiss their employees needed only to give due notice. After many years of service, therefore, an employee could be cast aside with only the week or two's notice laid down in his contract, and would have no legal ground for complaint whether his dismissal was for good reason or bad, or for no reason at all. These rules signally failed to inspire mutual confidence between employers and employees or to benefit industrial relations generally. In the 1960s Lord Donovan's Royal Commission Report on industrial relations in Britain found that nearly one third of our strikes resulted from alleged arbitrary dismissal or similar inconsiderate treatment of individual employees. It was clear that both sides would benefit from greater security of employment, and slowly but surely came fundamental changes in the law.

3.02 Notice

There were four main lines of reform, some much more important than others. The first tentative step was when the Contracts of Employment Act 1963 laid down requirements as to written particulars of employment, noted in Chapter 1. This Act was also of some significance in introducing minimum periods of notice, as now provided by sections 49 and 50 of the Employment Protection

(Consolidation) Act 1978. The rules as to notice benefit employees who have worked more than sixteen hours a week by contract for at least one month, or who have worked more than eight hours but less than sixteen hours a week for five years. It is important to note that hours are measured by contractual obligation, not by the number of hours actually worked. Overtime hours are therefore excluded, unless obligatory on both sides. Employees working the requisite number of hours by contract are entitled to at least one week's notice after the qualifying month (or after five years, as the case may be). That entitlement applies for two years, and then an additional week's notice must be given for every year of employment up to a maximum of twelve weeks after twelve years. These periods are not reciprocal. The employer is entitled only to one week's notice after the first month. A contract giving shorter periods than those in the Act is invalid to that extent, but if longer periods are agreed they are binding.

The employer may give money in lieu of notice, or conversely may agree to waive notice if the employee wishes to go immediately. In theory, an employee who leaves without giving notice and without his employer's agreement could be sued for damages for breach of contract. In practice, the more likely result would be refusal to give a reference.

While working out their statutory periods of notice, employees must be paid their normal weekly pay. If they are available for work but there is none to do, or if they are absent because of illness or injury or on holiday, they must still be paid for the requisite number of weeks. The amount due is calculated in accordance with the Act, as set out in Chapter 7 (see [7.13]). Sick pay is deducted from the resulting sum.

3.03 Unfair dismissal

The third advance in employment rights was the Redundancy Payments Act 1965. By requiring payment to be made on this one ground of dismissal, the Act made a major departure from the basic rule that employers incurred no liability if they dismissed with notice. The redundancy provisions are now stated in the

Employment Protection (Consolidation) Act 1978, as set out in Chapter 7. The fourth and by far the most important development was the introduction in the Industrial Relations Act 1971 of the concept of unfair dismissal. Effectively this new principle made a person's job an item of his or her property which could not be taken away without lawful excuse, and the giving or withholding of notice became correspondingly unimportant. Again, the rules are now to be found in the Employment Protection (Consolidation) Act. In the rest of this chapter we set out the conditions of entitlement to compensation for unfair dismissal, and in succeeding chapters explain how the rules work.

3.04   Qualifying service

The right to claim compensation for dismissal depends in the first place on length of service, age and occupation. In employment beginning before 1 June 1985, one year's service was necessary under a contract requiring more than sixteen hours a week, or alternatively five years' service under a contract requiring more than eight hours a week. If there were then twenty or fewer employees in an enterprise, the qualifying period was at least two years. For everyone starting work on or after 1 June 1985, however, the period of qualifying service is two years. An alternative qualification is five years' service under a contract for at least eight hours a week. Time starts to run from the date on which the employee begins work under the contract, and ends on the 'effective date of termination' [8.2].

Hours are calculated in the same way as for notice as shown above, i.e. according to what the contract actually lays down and not by average hours worked or time spent in preparation or, as a rule, on call. Once the requisite number of hours has been worked, no subsequent reduction in hours affects entitlement. Permitted absences from work, for holidays, sickness, etc., likewise do not affect entitlement, nor does the issue of a new contract if work can be regarded as continuous. Thus in *Ford* v. *Warwickshire C.C.* (1983) a teacher employed under eight successive years' contracts, each expiring with the summer vacation, was held continuously employed throughout the eight years (but see *B.B.C.* v. *Ioannou* (1975) below, as to the effect of fixed term contracts in this situation).

Continuity is not affected where a person is reinstated by tribunal order. Imposition of new terms on re-engagement does not of itself affect continuity: *Williams* v. *National Theatre* (1982). Time spent on strike does not count towards length of service. Questions of continuity and, in particular, the extent to which continuity is affected by a change of employer, are discussed further in the context of redundancy rights: see [7.10–7.12].

3.05   Discrimination

Employees dismissed within the first two (or five, as the case may be) years' service have as a rule no protection beyond their entitlement to notice, plus entitlement after six months' service to a written statement of the reasons for dismissal. (Employees who 'live in', however, may be entitled to longer periods of notice before having to leave the premises.) Major exceptions to the qualifying service rules arise when dismissal is on discriminatory grounds forbidden by law. Dismissal at any time because of sex, pregnancy (unless the woman is thereby disabled from doing her own or any suitable alternative work), or race, colour, nationality, ethnic or national origin is a civil wrong under the Sex Discrimination Act 1975 or Race Relations Act 1976. Protection against racial or ethnic discrimination may extend also to certain religious groups, e.g. Sikhs, but does not thereby entitle employees to time off for religious observances: *Ahmad* v. *I.L.E.A.* (1977). Compensation up to £8000 (1986–7 rates) may be awarded, including a sum for humiliation and distress.

Both of these Acts recognise that discrimination may be indirect as well as direct. Indirect discrimination occurs when a requirement or condition is imposed which though apparently equally applicable to all is such that in practice the number of persons of one sex or race able to comply with it is disproportionately small, and the requirement cannot otherwise be justified and is detrimental in effect. A 'requirement or condition' is a rule or bar which prevents appointment rather than an attitude or preference which makes it less likely: *Perera* v. *Civil Service Commission* (1983) – a conclusion which seems virtually to nullify the legislation. Examples in the race context include an unjustifiable requirement of a very short training period for a complicated job and an unnecessary upper age limit for admission to a training course – both of which were held to be more difficult for immigrants to comply with: *Bayoomi* v. *B.R.* (1981); *Perera* v. *Civil Service Commission*, above.

On the other hand, a requirement of good English for the writing of technical reports was upheld in *Chiu* v. *British Aerospace* (1982), as was a prerequisite of managerial experience for a management studies course: *Ojutiku* v. *Manpower Services Commission* (1981). Similarly in *Panesar* v. *Nestlé* (1972) a rule prohibiting long hair was held indirectly to discriminate against Sikhs but justified in the interests of safety and hygiene. *Raval* v. *D.H.S.S.* (1985) was a particularly vexed case. The complainant was a teacher who had qualified in Kenya. She applied for a clerical job in the D.H.S.S. but was refused because she did not have the requisite O-level pass in English language. The tribunal agreed that this was indirectly discriminatory but not detrimental to the complainant in that she could easily pass the examination. The Employment Appeal Tribunal rejected this argument but nonetheless accepted that the O-level requirement was justified (in the sense that it was a reasonable one, as distinct from being absolutely necessary). We observe also that even where the employee resigns this may still be seen as dismissal if resignation results from discriminatory pressure, e.g. sexual harassment, exerted or condoned by management: *Porcelli* v. *Strathclyde Regional Council* (1985).

Dismissal or other less favourable treatment because of trade union membership or non-membership is another form of discrimination, forbidden by the Employment Protection (Consolidation) Act. The position here is complicated by closed shop requirements which permit dismissal in circumstances described at the end of this chapter. Liability may also be incurred for dismissal in breach of the Rehabilitation of Offenders Act 1974. The object of this Act is to enable people to live down criminal conduct if they do not reoffend. It says that once a conviction is 'spent' it need not normally be disclosed, and dismissal or other discrimination because of a spent conviction or failure to disclose it is automatically unfair. The main rules are that convictions resulting in imprisonment for more than thirty months are never spent, while imprisonment for between six and thirty months is spent after ten years. The rehabilitation period for imprisonment up to six months is seven years, as also for youth custody. Convictions resulting in fines are spent after five years. A sentence of probation is spent after six months. The Act excludes people seeking public, legal or medical employment and various posts in financial services who must therefore disclose all convictions if so required. In Northern Ireland it is illegal also to discriminate on grounds of religious or political belief. If none of these Acts apply then, as we have said, dismissal with due notice and before the qualifying years of service have elapsed cannot be challenged at law, however arbitrary and prejudiced it might be.

3.06   Age limits and excluded occupations

The usual rule is that employees cannot claim compensation after reaching pensionable age – 60 for women and 65 for men – but this does not apply where the 'normal retiring age' is higher or lower than pensionable age: section 64. Tribunals have found it quite difficult to say what is meant by the 'normal' age, and still more so to apply the rule in particular cases. In *Waite* v. *G.C.H.Q.* (1983) the House of Lords explained that the first line of inquiry must be what the contract says about retirement. Only very exceptionally could some age other than that stated in the contract be the 'normal' one. Their Lordships accepted nonetheless that custom and practice in a particular employment might lead to some contrary conclusions. But if there is no provision to the contrary, express or implied, then the statutory retirement ages apply.

Hughes v. *D.H.S.S.* (1985), again a House of Lords decision, says that what is 'normal' for a given employee is what he is entitled to expect under his contracts – and so if at some point in his working life the employer changes the retirement age the employee's expectation must change accordingly. How far employers are in fact free to change retirement ages unilaterally remains doubtful; part of the problem in *Hughes* was that the terms originally agreed, including the age of retirement, had been expressed merely as matters of departmental convenience. That enabled their Lordships to say that the higher retirement age which the employee originally expected was effective only while the departmental circular in question remained in force. When a change in policy was communicated to the relevant employees, any reasonable expectations they might have had from previous circulars were destroyed and replaced by others prescribed by the new circular.

Employees excluded altogether from the Employment Protection (Consolidation) Act's protection against unfair dismissal are registered dock workers (who are protected instead by regulations made under the Dock Workers (Regulation of Employment) Act 1946), police and prison officers, fishermen paid by profit-sharing, and employees who normally work abroad: section 141. In this latter connection the Court of Appeal said in *Janata Bank* v. *Ahmed* (1981) that a 'broad brush' approach was necessary to determine where a person normally worked. It was not just a matter of deciding where he was normally based, or what the contract said – though these were most important indications. The question was whether employment here or abroad was essentially a temporary posting, or a basic change in the contract. How, where and by whom was the employee paid? What National Insurance arrangements were made? All are relevant lines of inquiry. Employees are deemed to work in Great Britain if they work on ships registered here, unless their work takes them wholly outside the country or they are not ordinarily resident here, and so are those who work within British territorial waters (up to three miles from shore), or on offshore installations such as North Sea oil rigs. Employees are also unable to claim if they work under fixed term contracts of one year or more and agree in writing not to claim compensation for unfair dismissal as and when the term expires: section 142. (See also [3.11] below.)

THE MEANING OF DISMISSAL

3.07   Voluntary termination

No claim can be made unless there has been a dismissal as defined in the 1978 Act, below. Not all partings of the ways necessarily involve dismissal. The employee may leave voluntarily, or when the job he was taken on to do is completed, or because of a dispute or misunderstanding with his employer. Supervening events may make it impossible to fulfil the contract. None of these circumstances in themselves amount to dismissal.

An employee may agree to go but still change his mind and sue. The employer will then have to prove that his agreement was indeed voluntary and not made under pressure. So, for example, in *University of Liverpool* v. *Birch* (1984) the employer had to convince the tribunal that after circulating details of an early retirement scheme he did not dismiss an employee who applied for early retirement and was then asked formally to resign.

Problems of this kind have arisen where employees have been required to sign undertakings not to overstay their holidays and acknowledging that if they do overstay they will lose their jobs. If the employee does not return on time has he thereby agreed to termination of his contract? Such 'agreements', while apparently sensible precautions on the employer's part against absenteeism, are open to abuse. The employee may not appreciate the significance of what he is required to sign, and rigid enforcement may not take proper account of circumstances beyond the employee's control. There have been cases both ways, but the prevailing view as expressed by the Employment Appeal Tribunal in *Igbo* v. *Johnson Matthey* (1985) is that employees who sign clear and unambiguous documents stating that failure to return to work on a given day after a holiday will result in automatic termination of employment, and who understand what they are signing, will almost certainly be deemed to have agreed to termination in these circumstances. The employee in *Igbo* lost her claim even though her late return was in fact due to illness.

Employers sometimes encourage unwanted employees to leave by giving them good references. This seems a most misguided practice. It exposes the employer to a claim for damages for negligent advice by any subsequent employer, and if by any chance the employee does not 'go quietly', the favourable reference will undermine the employer's case against him.

It has been argued that certain kinds of gross misconduct may be interpreted as 'self-dismissal'. In *Gannon* v. *Firth* (1976), for example, employees who walked off a job without warning or justification and who thereby created serious dangers for others were held to have repudiated their contracts and thus 'dismissed themselves'. But more recent cases reject the view that dangerous or irresponsible behaviour necessarily brings the contract to an end. Tribunals prefer to leave it to the employer to decide whether or not to 'accept' such behaviour as repudiation. He 'accepts' by dismissing, and in that way the burden of proof is more clearly established. An example is *Rasool* v. *Hepworth* (1980). The men were warned they would be in breach of contract if they attended a mass meeting in works time. They duly attended the meeting. It was held that their disobedience did not of itself end their contracts, but that their subsequent dismissals for disobedience were fair. Similarly, in *Pendlebury* v. *Christian Schools* (1985) where it was argued that the contract had been terminated by each side's misunderstanding of the other's conduct, the Employment Appeal Tribunal said categorically that contracts of employment could only be ended by the employer's express or implied acceptance of the employee's breach or resignation as bringing the contract to an end.

Again, what is said or done as between employer and employee may be misinterpreted, and if an employee leaves believing he has been sacked when investigation of the facts shows he has not, he will have no claim. There have been several cases, for example, on the precise meaning and effect of common forms of industrial back-chat such as that in *Futty* v. *Brekkes* (1974). This case concerned a discussion between a foreman and a fish filleter on Hull docks, which ended with the foreman telling the filleter: 'If you don't like the job you can fuck off'. The employee took him at his word, left the job and claimed compensation for unfair dismissal. The tribunal therefore had to decide what exactly the foreman meant. It was held that the effect of his message was: 'If you are complaining about the fish you are working on, or the quality of it, or if you do not like what in fact you are doing, then you can leave your work, clock off, and you will be paid up to the time when you do so. Then you can come back when you are disposed to start work again the next day'. On that interpretation there was therefore no dismissal but only, as the tribunal put it, a 'general exhortation'. It followed from this masterpiece of compression that the employee left without good reason and so lost his claim. A somewhat similar case was *Stern* v. *Simpson* (1983) which turned on the precise significance to be attached to the words: 'Go, get out, get out!'

Warning an employee of impending closure or advising him to seek a job elsewhere, but not actually telling him to resign or that he will be dismissed, does not constitute dismissal. There must be a specified or ascertainable date on which employment is to end: *Haseltine Lake* v. *Dowler* (1981). And even after the most unambiguous dismissal the employer may still wish to reconsider the matter and must be allowed to change his mind, unless the employee has already acted on the termination: *Martin* v. *Yeoman* (1983). The same applies also to a 'spur of the moment' resignation by the employee.

Another possibility is that circumstances might change so as to make it impossible or impracticable to carry out the contract. If so it is 'frustrated' and brought to an end by law, not by any action on the employer's part. There could then be no question of liability upon him. Unfortunately, the application of the rules of frustration to contracts of employment is uncertain. Events such as long-term illness or injury have occasionally been regarded as frustrating the contract – *Marshall* v. *Harland & Wolff* (1972) – but on the other hand the tribunal might ask why, if the employer thought the contract could not be fulfilled, he did not see fit to dismiss the absent employee: *Hart* v. *Marshall* (1977). Accidental destruction of the employer's premises would no doubt be accepted as frustrating the contract. An employee's conviction and imprisonment might appear to have the same effect, but since these events are brought about by the employee himself the rules might not apply: *Norris* v. *Southampton C.C.* (1982).

In practice, as we said above, the tribunals prefer to regard any deliberate conduct by the employee which seriously affects his performance of the contract as repudiatory, leaving the employer to respond by dismissal if he so wishes. And even in illness cases they prefer the employer to take the initiative and give notice in accordance with the contract: *Harman* v. *Flexible Lamps* (1980). On the whole that seems the safest policy for the employer.

3.08   Termination by employer

Section 55 of the 1978 Act provides three definitions of dismissal, one or other of which must be established before a claim can be considered:

(1) The employer may end the contract himself, with or without notice.
(2) The employee may end the contract, with or without notice, when justified in ending it without notice because of the employer's conduct.
(3) A person employed under a fixed term contract is dismissed when the term expires and the contract is not renewed.

Termination by the employer is the commonest form of dismissal, and its simplest expression is probably 'You're fired!' The circumstances in which the employer is justified in taking this course are examined at length in subsequent chapters, but essentially require him to prove that the employee is incapable of doing his work, or has misconducted himself, or that his continued employment would be against the law, or that the employee is redundant, or that there is some other substantial reason justifying dismissal. If notice is given in circumstances which make dismissal unfair the employee can start proceedings against his employer before notice expires.

3.09   Constructive dismissal

As regards the second definition of dismissal given above, an employee's resignation in response to his employer's conduct is known as 'constructive' (i.e. indirect or imputed) dismissal. It is convenient to examine this concept more fully at this point. The most straightforward example of involuntary resignation would be: 'Resign or I will sack you'. But there are infinite variations, and the pressures are not always so obvious. The onus of proving this form of dismissal is upon the employee, and can be a difficult one to discharge. The question facing the tribunal is in effect: 'Did he fall or was he pushed?' To prove he was 'pushed', the employee must establish that his employer had previously repudiated the contract of employment. It is not sufficient for him simply to show he was not happy at work or did not like the way things were going.

The leading case on constructive dismissal is *Western Excavating* v. *Sharp* (1978). The employee here was suspended without pay for misconduct and as a result got into financial difficulties. He asked his employer for a loan or for his holiday pay to help him out. When the employer refused he resigned. His claim that he had no alternative was rejected, because the employer's refusal did not amount to a breach or repudiation of his contract. The law's requirements were explained as follows by Lord Denning in the Court of Appeal:

> 'If the employer is guilty of conduct which is a significant breach going to the root of the contract of employment, or which shows that the employer no longer intends to be bound by one or more of the essential terms of the contract, then the employee is entitled to treat himself as discharged from any further performance. If he does so, then he terminates the contract by reason of the employer's conduct. He is constructively dismissed. The employee is entitled in those circumstances to leave at the instant without giving any notice at all or, alternatively, he may give notice and say that he is leaving at the end of the notice. But the conduct must in either case be sufficiently serious to entitle him to leave at once.'

It may be very difficult for the employee to prove breach of any particular term of the contract. Essentially his complaint may be that the employer is behaving unreasonably. The tribunals and courts may still be willing to help him by saying, as we saw in Chapter 2, that employers are contractually obliged to behave with reasonable consideration for their employees' well-being, consistently with the express terms of the contract. In *Woods* v. *W.M. Car Services* (1981), for example, it was said that deliberate harassment of an employee would justify his or her resignation, though in this particular case a new employer's insistence on lower pay, longer hours and more onerous duties were all held to be permissible in the circumstances. In *Dutton* v. *Daly* (1985), where the employee left because of allegedly inadequate safety precautions, the E.A.T. said the question was simply whether the employer had behaved reasonably – a more direct line of inquiry but one incompatible with *Western Excavating*, above.

There are many cases to illustrate where the tribunals draw the line, even though we cannot say with any certainty where they might draw it in the future on any particular set of facts. As regards unacceptably inconsiderate behaviour by employers, examples include completely unfounded accusations of theft (*Robinson* v. *Crompton Parkinson* (1978)); gross incivility (*I.O.W. Tourist Board* v. *Coombes* (1976) – where the employer said his secretary was 'an intolerable bitch every Monday morning'); failure to support a newly appointed supervisor (*A.T.S.* v. *Waterhouse* (1977)); ending an employee's training programme because of union intimidation (*Callanan* v. *Surrey Area Health Authority* (1980)); treating a long-serving employee like an office boy (*Garner* v. *Grange* (1977)). In *P.O.* v. *Roberts* (1980) the employee resigned after being refused a transfer, and after discovering that she had been given a false explanation instead of being told of a bad report upon her. The employer's conduct here was held to be in breach of his duty to maintain mutual trust and confidence.

Laying off or suspending an employee may amount to breach of contract by the employer, depending on duration, unless in accordance with the express or implied terms of the contract. Demotion may be an appropriate penalty for a disciplinary offence, but otherwise will probably justify a claim for constructive dismissal, even if only temporary (*Millbrook* v. *McIntosh* (1981); *McNeil* v. *Crimin* (1984)). Exposing an employee to unnecessary danger or other intolerable working conditions such as extreme heat or cold also justifies resignation: *Oxley* v. *Firth* (1980). If he can establish a fundamental breach the employee is under no obligation to use the employer's grievance procedure to try to solve the problem.

These cases may be contrasted with others where the employee could prove only that he had a grievance, but not that it arose from anything more than dissatisfaction with conditions of employment or the kind of reverse or criticism normal in working life. In *Spencer* v. *McCowan* (1975), for instance, an employee was refused a periodic wage review, suffered the 'indignity' of having a younger man promoted over him, was told his work must improve and warned of possible redundancies. The tribunal held that none of these incidents separately or cumulatively amounted to dismissal, though it did accept that repeated refusal to review wages might have that effect. A similar case is *Walker* v. *Wedgwood* (1978), where the employee was neither consulted over the appointment of a subordinate nor told of subordinates' pay increases when his own pay was held down. Here again it was held that the employer had not repudiated the contract and so the employee lost his claim for constructive dismissal. Reference might also be made to *B.L.* v. *McQuilken* (1978) (see [1.8]) where it will be recalled that the employee unsuccessfully alleged breach of a collective agreement as a ground for resignation.

3.10   Changing the terms: the right to manage

A particularly vexed issue as regards constructive dismissal is whether or to what extent the employer has a right to vary the terms of the contract. To the extent that the employer has such a right, any employee resigning in protest is bound to lose his claim. We have argued before that as a matter of principle an employer must be able to initiate and compel acceptance of *certain* changes in the terms of employment (just as unions may demand and insist upon new terms regarding pay, hours, etc.) – but it is virtually impossible to say how far employers' powers go in this respect.

   If we take a basic provision such as the rate of pay we can see that a continued wilful refusal to pay due wages or a substantial and unilateral change in conditions of entitlement must appear as a fundamental breach of contract, and as such give rise to a claim for compensation for constructive dismissal (and/or to a claim for lost pay in the county court). So in *Hill* v. *Mooney* (1981) ending at 1 per cent commission payment was held to be repudiatory, as was loss of use of a company car in *Moore* v. *Winn* (1975). But if there is good reason for non-payment, e.g. a cash flow problem, the employee may be expected to wait and see if it can be resolved: *Adams* v. *Zub* (1978). And if the reduction is a very small one, in the interests perhaps of introducing a more rational wages structure, it might have to be accepted: *Gilbert* v. *Goldstone* (1977). Each case must be considered on its own merits.

   The same is true of other, possibly still more far-reaching

changes in working conditions. There may be no doubt that the effect of the change is that the employer is in breach of contract, but he is still not necessarily liable for his employee's resignation. A balance has somehow to be struck between sanctity of contract and management's right to respond to changing economic circumstances – or else go out of business. The tribunals are generally reluctant to interfere with a person's right to run his own business as he sees fit, subject to the law of the land, if they are convinced that the changes he brings about are those demanded of him by 'sound, good business reasons', as the Court of Appeal put it in *Hollister* v. *National Farmers' Union* (1979). The same sentiment was expressed by Lord Justice Watkins in *Woods* v. *W.M. Car Services* (1981): 'Employers should not be put in a position where through the wrongful refusal of their employees to accept change, they are prevented from introducing improved business methods'.

The point is clearly made by *Brandon* v. *Murphy* (1983), where employees at a small bakery were required in breach of their national agreement to work on New Year's Day in order to meet a demand by the employer's largest customer over the holiday season. They were offered other holidays in lieu. An employee who refused to accept this variation in his contract was held fairly dismissed because of the necessity of the situation. Longer term and more fundamental changes may be equally essential, as illustrated by *Yusuf* v. *Aberplace* (1985). Because of falling demand the company here reduced its employees' weekly hours from sixty to forty-four, and introduced a seven-day working rota. The employees had previously received overtime payments for weekend work, but these were now abolished. Those who refused were held to have been fairly dismissed – and evidently the same conclusion would follow if they had resigned instead.

Similarly in *Johnson* v. *Nottinghamshire Police Authority* (1974) employers were held entitled to require a clerk to move from a five-day week to a six-day shift system – though a change from night shift to day shift without the employee's agreement was essentially a different job and so led to liability for dismissal in *Squibb* v. *Shepperton Studios* (1974). Withdrawal of a fringe benefit – free travel – on grounds of economic necessity was held in *Durrant* v. *Clariston* (1974) to be a breach of contract by the employer but one for which he could not be blamed. Changes agreed with a union are the more likely to be upheld. Other cases on the same lines are discussed in the context of dismissal for disobedience: see [5.05].

Does the employer's right to compel acceptance of change extend to changes in the nature of the job itself, as distinct from more peripheral issues of pay, hours, holidays and the like? This is undoubtedly the most vexed aspect of the question, and once again, regrettably, there are no categorical answers. In theory we can say that an employee taken on to do job X ought not to be required to do job Y, and if he is required to do it, refuses and is dismissed, directly or constructively, he ought then to succeed in his claim – unless, of course, his contract expressly or impliedly provides for mobility or transferability. In practice, however, it seems all a matter of degree, expediency and again economic pressure, which makes the outcome very uncertain.

Genower v. *Ealing Area Health Authority* (1980) is a good example of the problem. The applicant was employed as a general administrative assistant at one of the respondent's hospitals, purchasing and distributing medical and surgical equipment. His contract specified these duties and said that he might be called upon to do work within this job description at other hospitals within the group. To avoid the dangers of bribery and corruption it was the Authority's policy not to leave employees at his level in charge of one department for too long a period. In due course, Mr Genower was told to go to the provisions and direct order section of another hospital – which he saw as a different type of job. He thought this would be a complete waste of his specialised knowledge and experience of medical and surgical equipment. Left, as he saw it, with no alternative, he resigned and sued for compensation for constructive dismissal. The Employment Appeal Tribunal observed that many people's terms of employment were such as to enable them to be moved from one post to another without any breach of contract. Here, however, the Tribunal agreed that the change did indeed represent a '*fundamental breach*'. The employers 'were proposing to transfer him to something which was *quite outside the terms of his employment*' (author's italics). On the face of it, therefore, he was being required to do a different job and so should have been able to refuse without being penalised.

The Authority had to justify its fundamental breach of Mr

Genower's contract. There were no grounds for complaint against him, nor was he redundant. The only remaining ground on which the Authority might escape liability was by proving 'some other substantial reason' for dismissing him, as provided by section 57 of the 1978 Act. Did they have such a reason? He was required to move because of the danger of fraud. As between employer and employee, who must decide how the problem should be tackled? Was this particular solution a fair and reasonable one? If the answer is that the solution must be negotiated, i.e. meet with the employee's approval, then that would deny management's right to decide how to tackle the problem, since the employee might not approve. We should bear in mind also that it is usually management which is the victim of fraud, not its employees. The E.A.T. cited *Hollister's* case, above, and held that the Authority had a 'sound, good business reason' for its policy which was in turn a 'substantial reason' for the constructive dismissal. It followed that the Authority was not liable, despite its deliberate and fundamental breach.

This conclusion remains surprising, and can probably only be justified on a choice-of-evils basis. A right to override contractual obligations so completely is obviously open to abuse, much as unions and employees abuse their economic power whenever they break collective agreements and disregard agreed procedures. On the other hand, employers must be free to safeguard their businesses. In practice, negotiation and compromise – while not obligatory (see [5.06]) – are more likely to achieve results than compulsion, but we see that compulsion may sometimes be an acceptable last resort. We might suppose also that the tribunal found it easier to reach their decision in *Genower* because the two jobs were of a broadly similar nature, although they did not specifically say so. We must bear in mind also that if the job content is changed too much the employee will probably be unable to do the job properly, but to sack him then for incapacity would be patently unfair.

Not many cases go as far as *Genower*, but we should note the Court of Appeal decision in *Savoia* v. *Chiltern Herb Farms* (1982). For reasons of efficiency, the employee here was not allowed to return to his old job after illness but refused his employer's instruction to take a medical examination to determine his suitability for a new one. He resigned, but lost his claim. This again suggests an obligation to take on a new job.

Illustrations of the numerous decisions going the other way include *Pedersen* v. *Camden London Borough Council* (1981). Mr Pedersen was employed primarily as a bar steward but with subsidiary duties as catering assistant. Work on the bar declined and he was required to spend almost all his time on catering duties. His claim for constructive dismissal arising from this change in emphasis was successful. The outcome was the same in *Wadham Stringer* v. *Brown* (1983), where a fleet sales director was moved to an inadequate office and gradually required to work as a retail salesman. We have seen that changes such as these leading to demotion are very risky from the employer's point of view, and are likely to be justifiable only as disciplinary measures. Even then, employers should consider very carefully whether the resulting loss of status, pay and prospects is not too severe a penalty for the offence in question. If it is it may well give rise to a claim for constructive dismissal.

A dispute in good faith as to the interpretation of a contract does not of itself justify resignation – *Wright* v. *Punch* (1980) – though that could leave the employee in difficulties because eventually he might have no other way of proving the validity of his argument. Resigning by mutual agreement cannot give rise to a claim for constructive dismissal, even where as noted earlier the employer formally asks for resignation in order to fulfil early retirement procedures, or where the employee chooses to resign rather than face disciplinary proceedings: *Staffordshire C.C.* v. *Donovan* (1981). On the other hand, the fact that the employee asks to leave before notice expires does not mean he has freely agreed to go.

There must of course *be* a resignation before any claim can be made, since one cannot both remain at work and say one has been dismissed. Delay in resigning will not help a constructive dismissal claim, but if the employee makes it clear he is staying on under protest and does not stay too long he may still be able to claim when he goes. In *Cox* v. *Crook* (1981) the employee lost his claim because he did not resign until seven months after the incidents in dispute.

3.11   Non-renewal of fixed term contracts

The third form of dismissal is non-renewal of a fixed term contract. A fixed term contract is one stated to last for a particular length of time. It has a 'defined beginning and a defined end' as was said in *Wiltshire C.C.* v. *N.A.T.F.H.E.* (1980) where a teacher's contract for the academic year was held to be a fixed term contract. It is immaterial that such a contract may allow for earlier termination by notice or because of misconduct, incapacity, etc. A contract for a particular purpose or enterprise, e.g. to build a house or repair a ship, however, is not for a fixed term. It ends whenever the task is completed, and so there is no dismissal according to law: *Ryan* v. *Shipboard Maintenance* (1980). A training or probationary period specified in a contract does not of itself confer fixed term rights.

Although the expiry and non-renewal of a fixed term contract is classified as dismissal, that does not resolve the separate question of whether such a dismissal is fair. On the face of it dismissal in these circumstances *is* fair, if and insofar as it was the basis of understanding between employer and employee that the contract would come to an end on the given date. Section 142 of the 1978 Act underlines this view by enabling employers who offer fixed term contracts of one year or more to ask for employees' written agreement not to claim compensation for unfair dismissal or redundancy as and when the term expires. If an employee is dismissed before then, however, he may still make a claim.

Before deciding what may or may not be fair when a fixed term contract ends we should note that the rule is concerned only with renewal of existing contracts, not with granting altogether new and different ones. In many cases, the existing contract cannot be renewed. When a contract of apprenticeship or other form of training ends, for example, there can be no question of granting a new training contract. What the newly qualified employee wants is an entirely different kind of contract which recognises his new status. But so far as the law is concerned an employee has no special right to be taken on in a different or more highly paid capacity when his training or other fixed term employment ends, nor any particular priority over other candidates for the job for which he has trained. The problem has arisen for locums in the Health Service, among others. The legal position in such cases was clearly established in *Gwent C.C.* v. *Lane* (1978), where the Employment Appeal Tribunal said:

> 'While we accept that consideration for the needs of the employee should be given according to what is proper in the circumstances, it seems to us that there is a danger if the duty is pitched too high, that the reasonable discretion of the appointing body or committee or sub-committee will be unduly hampered and that the recruitment of new blood will be unreasonably restricted. In particular we feel that the industrial tribunal were not right when they said that before other posts were advertised the claims of the temporary employee should be considered, and that if he were suitable he should have been engaged in preference to advertising the post generally. This appears to amount to a rule that a comparatively short-term temporary employee whose contract has not been renewed has some kind of right to priority of appointment to an available suitable post over and above any other suitable candidate. We think that this is going too far. Certainly, we think that even if in a particular case the circumstances seem to justify such a conclusion, it would require careful examination of the evidence to see what the practical consequences of such a rule would be.'

The chances of an employee succeeding on a non-renewal claim are thus quite small. Employers should, however, beware of exposing themselves to liability by leading employees to believe their contracts will be renewed or by keeping employees on beyond the date of expiry, so that their contracts are or seem to be of indefinite duration.

It is not altogether certain whether an employee who wishes to challenge this form of dismissal can link together a series of short fixed term contracts to establish the necessary continuity of service, or whether he is confined to the most recent contract. *Ford* v. *Warwickshire C.C.* (1983) took the former view. *B.B.C.* v. *Ioannou* (1975) the latter. *Ford*'s case seems the more realistic in accepting continuity where the contracts are regularly renewed.

The courts are of course aware that short fixed term contracts are now very common and that employers may misuse them in order to avoid liability for unfair dismissal. In *Terry* v. *East Sussex C.C.*

(1976) the E.A.T. said:

> 'The great thing is to make sure that the case is a genuine one; for industrial tribunals to hold a balance. On the one hand, employers who have a genuine need for fixed term employment, which can be seen from the outset not to be ongoing, need to be protected. On the other hand, employees have to be protected against being deprived of their rights through ordinary employments being dressed up in the form of temporary fixed term contracts.'

These cautionary words were echoed and endorsed by the Court of Appeal in *North Yorkshire C.C.* v. *Fay* (1985). Employers may therefore expect to be asked to justify their adoption of this particular kind of contract.

3.12   The meaning of 'fairness'

What is 'fairness'? This is, of course, the crucial question. In seeking to answer it the law has somehow to reconcile the conflicting interests of employer and employee. It tries to fulfil this (well-nigh impossible) task first by requiring the employer to show good cause for dismissal. Under section 57 of the 1978 Act, dismissal is unfair unless the employer can prove that the employee was incapable of doing his job properly, or had misconducted himself, or that it was illegal to continue to employ him, or that he was redundant, or that there was 'some other substantial reason' for his dismissal. The tribunal must then be satisfied that it was reasonable to dismiss on such grounds – a question to be resolved as section 57 says 'in accordance with equity and the substantial merits of the case'. This in turn requires consideration of any injustice suffered by the employee, and a final attempt to balance that against the operating needs of the employer: *Dobie* v. *Burns* (1984).

Guidelines as to fairness are offered by the ACAS Code of Practice on disciplinary practice and procedures, discussed in [6.03] and reproduced in Appendix 2. The draft of the revised and enlarged form of the Code appears in Appendix 3. It is important to remember that the Code is not legally binding. Compliance or non-compliance is merely evidence for the tribunal to take into account one way or the other as to the fairness of any particular dismissal.

What is fair therefore depends almost entirely upon the merits of the particular case – but as seen by whom? Who is to decide, for example, on the necessary degree or extent of incapacity or misconduct? Should the tribunal with its independent lawyer-chairman and CBI and TUC nominees impose its own standards, or accept those of industry with which it may not necessarily agree? After some initial vacillation, the answer now accepted is that the tribunal finds the facts on which the employer's decision was based and then decides whether dismissal was a reasonable response to them; not, in other words, whether it would itself have dismissed on those grounds. The distinction is a most important one. It means that tribunals are not there to set higher external standards, but to ensure due observance of existing employment norms. The situation was explained as follows in two leading cases: first, the Employment Appeal Tribunal's decision in *Rolls-Royce* v. *Walpole* (1980):

> 'In a given set of circumstances, it is possible for two perfectly reasonable employers to take a different course of action in relation to an employee. Frequently there is a range of responses to the conduct or capacity of an employee on the part of the employer, from and including summary dismissal downwards to a mere informal warning, which can be said to be reasonable. It is precisely because this range of possible responses does exist in many cases that it is neither for the E.A.T. on an appeal, nor for an industrial tribunal on the original hearing, to substitute its respective views for those of the particular employer concerned.'

This was endorsed by the Court of Appeal in *British Leyland* v. *Swift* (1981):

> 'The correct test is: was it reasonable for the employer to dismiss him? If no reasonable employer would have dismissed him, then the dismissal is unfair. But if a reasonable employer might reasonably have dismissed him, then the dismissal is fair. It must

be remembered that in all these cases there is a band of reasonableness, within which one employer might reasonably take one view; another quite reasonably take a different view ... If it was quite reasonable to dismiss him, then the dismissal must be upheld as fair: even though some other employers may not have dismissed him.'

The consequences of this line of inquiry, of asking whether dismissal is '*within the band of reasonable responses of a reasonable employer*', are very far-reaching for both parties. From the employee's point of view, while strictly he need not prove more than the fact of dismissal in order to launch his claim, it must still be very difficult to persuade a tribunal that 'no reasonable employer' would have dismissed him. From the employer's point of view the burden of disproving liability is reduced accordingly. All he needs is a good *prima facie* case, i.e. that in the light of the information reasonably available to him at the time (which presupposes some appropriate level of inquiry (see [6.02])) his decision to dismiss was a reasonable one.

FAIRNESS PREDETERMINED BY LAW

3.13   (1) Union membership

In a few exceptional cases the burden of proof is lifted from the employer and the fairness or otherwise of dismissal is laid down by law. The main exception concerns dismissal on ground of trade union membership or non-membership. Sections 58(1) and 59 of the 1978 Act state that dismissal or selection for redundancy must be unfair if based on the employee's membership or proposed membership of an independent trade union or his taking part or proposing to take part in the activities of such a union at an appropriate time, or conversely upon the fact that he was not a member or refused to become or remain a member.

An independent union is one which is not subject to an employer's control, financially or otherwise, and which has been approved as such by the Certification Officer appointed under the

Employment Protection Act 1975. An 'appropriate time' for taking part in its activities may be either outside working hours or within them and on the employer's premises, subject to the employer's express or implied consent. Where there is a closed shop agreement, only members of unions covered by the agreement are entitled to use the employer's premises for union purposes.

Guidance as to the scope of 'union activities' within this rule is given by the ACAS Code on time off for trade union duties. The Code says that union officials should be given reasonable time off (with pay) to attend policy and executive meetings in their representative capacities, while members should be able to vote and attend urgent union meetings – again subject where practicable to management's approval. Permission is not required for activities such as collecting union dues and canvassing for the union during one's lunch hour.

Union activities for present purposes do not include 'industrial action'. A distinction must also be drawn between union activities and disruptive actions by individual members. A doubtful example is *Chant* v. *Aquaboats* (1978), where petitioning against unsafe machinery was held not to be a union activity and so outside the statutory protection. The task of both management and the law in drawing the line here is even more delicate than usual. While the Code urges employers to cooperate with unions, 'the special protection afforded [to unions] must not be allowed to operate as a cloak or an excuse for conduct which may ordinarily justify dismissal': *Lyon* v. *St. James Press* (1976).

A case worthy of note here is *Therm-a-Stor* v. *Atkins* (1983). The employer arbitrarily dismissed twenty newly appointed employees because of their union's request for recognition. The Court of Appeal held they were not protected against this 'indefensible reaction' by section 58 because dismissal arose from their union's activities and not their own membership of it. Since they had not served long enough to be protected against unfair dismissal they were thus entirely without redress. The decision is remarkable, not least in the way it proves to employees the need for strong trade unions.

3.14 (2) The closed shop

The second situation in which the law declares in advance what is fair and what is not is in connection with membership of a closed shop. A pre- or post-entry closed shop is brought about by a 'union membership agreement'. This is defined in section 30 of the Labour government's Trade Union and Labour Relations Act 1974 as any agreement or arrangement made or existing between an employer or employers and a union or unions, requiring particular employees to belong to one or more specified independent unions. It will be appreciated that this is a very flexible definition. It accepts custom and practice and pressure and makes no reference at all to the wishes of the majority or how they are to be ascertained. In the Labour government's day the only lawful ground for exemption from membership once such an agreement or arrangement existed was that of religious objection. This was condemned as an undue restriction on freedom of choice by the European Court of Human Rights, and sections 58 and 58A of the 1978 Act as they now stand are the result of Conservative amendment of the Act by their 1980 and 1982 Employment Acts.

The present position as stated in section 58(3) is that where it is the practice for employees to belong to a particular union in accordance with an 'approved' union membership agreement, it is on principle, and subject to the following major exceptions, fair to sack employees who refuse to join. To establish a practice it is not necessary to show that almost all employees are members, nor that they have joined voluntarily, nor that their contracts require them to join, but certainly the level of membership must be 'substantial': *Taylor* v. *Cooperative Retail Services* (1982).

An agreement is 'approved' if, within the five years preceding the dismissal, it has been endorsed by at least 80 per cent of the employees affected by it, (or 85 per cent of those voting, unless the agreement took effect after 14 August 1980,) voting in a secret ballot, and there has been no subsequent contrary vote. For dismissal purposes, therefore, the Act in effect requires support for a closed shop to be tested every five years, and so very substantially modifies the definition in section 30 above. Employers may not wish to rouse this particular 'hornets' nest', but risk liability otherwise.

Against this presumption of fair dismissal we must now set the various grounds for exemption listed in section 58. If any of these apply, dismissal automatically becomes unfair. Shortly stated, employees are protected against dismissal (i) where they have conscientious (including religious) objections to joining a union, or (ii) deeply held personal convictions against joining (e.g. because of sincere differences of political opinion, or the belief that the union does not adequately represent their interests); (iii) where they were not required to join a union on first starting work and have not subsequently joined; (iv) where after a secret ballot in which they were eligible to vote and which approved a closed shop they did not join that or any union; (v) where they have taken or are taking legal action against the union because of unreasonable exclusion or expulsion from it; (vi) where professionally qualified employees are subject to written codes of conduct which would be broken if they went on strike, and for that reason they refuse to join a union; (vii) where on any of these grounds they refuse to make payments which may be required of them, e.g. to a charity, in lieu of membership.

Employees alleging dismissal because of union membership or non-membership or specifically because of closed shop requirements may claim 'interim relief' under section 77. The claim must be made within seven days of dismissal taking effect and in appropriate cases be supported by a union official's certificate as to the nature of the complaint. Unless the employer agrees to reinstate the employee or re-engage him on acceptable terms the tribunal will order that the contract of employment remain in existence, thus safeguarding rights to pay and other benefits, until the dismissal claim itself is heard.

A final most important consideration is that if dismissal for non-membership is brought about by threats of industrial action, the party making the threats may be personally liable to pay a greatly increased level of compensation. This point is dealt with more fully in [9.05].

3.15 (3) Strike action

We shall discuss the rights and wrongs of dismissal arising out of strike action more fully in [5.10]. In the meantime, we note in passing the importance of the rule in section 62 of the 1978 Act, which makes it by definition *fair* to dismiss employees while they are on strike, or locked out, so long as they are not victimised by the re-employment of some but not others within the following three months. But dismissal during a strike is not the only possible response, as [5.10] makes clear.

3.16   (4) Pregnancy

Section 60 of the 1978 Act makes it automatically unfair to dismiss an employee because she is pregnant, unless by the time dismissal takes effect she cannot do her work properly or in accordance with the law. Even if she is disabled in this way, dismissal is still unfair if the employer fails to offer any suitable alternative employment which may be available.

3.17   (5) National security

The final statutory provision on fairness is that contained in Schedule 9 of the Consolidation Act: a dismissal certified by a Minister of the Crown to be on grounds of national security cannot be challenged before a tribunal. Dismissal in these circumstances must therefore be accepted as fair.

These various predeterminations of fairness do not in as many words include dismissals arising out of discrimination on grounds of race or sex or in breach of the Rehabilitation of Offenders Act, above, but a finding of unfairness would appear inevitable in such cases.

3.18   Remedies

Having now discussed the basic principles of unfair dismissal it remains only to outline the remedies open to the former employee if he wins his claim. We describe them more fully in Chapter 9. In the first place the employee may claim up to two weeks' pay if the employer fails to provide an adequate or accurate written statement of the reasons for dismissal. This right arises after the first six months' service: section 53. But his most important remedy, at least in theory (see [3.19]), is an order for reinstatement in the previous job, or re-engagement on new terms in that or other employment, depending on what is practicable. If the employer wilfully disregards such an order, he may be ordered to pay up to £8060 (1986-7 rate) to the employee, as well as the basic and compensatory awards which are, in fact, the most common remedies. The maximum rates of these awards for 1986–7 are respectively £4650 and £8000. And if dismissal arises out of an employee's refusal to join a closed shop and is found unfair because he has one or other of the grounds of exemption mentioned above, the tribunal may make a further special award of up to £22,000 wholly or partly payable by the union.

3.19   The figures

Before we consider at length the precise grounds on which dismissals may be upheld, there is perhaps one final reflection which management may find helpful. In the writer's opinion, the effect of the new law of dismissal has been much misunderstood. Many employers seem to have assumed that 'you can't dismiss anyone nowadays', whatever the grounds for complaint. The reality of the matter is perhaps most clearly demonstrated by the following figures for dismissal cases decided or settled in 1983, the last year for which figures were available at the time of writing.

According to the Department of Employment's *Gazette*, just over 30,000 dismissal claims were dealt with in 1983. Nearly 20,000 were withdrawn or settled by conciliation. In the 10,000 or so conciliated cases the median amount of compensation was £421. Of the total of nearly 10,400 cases reaching industrial tribunals, 7082 were rejected. These included 4484 held to be fair dismissals, and the rest were found invalid or withdrawn at the last moment. Only 3299 claims, 11 per cent of the year's total, were upheld. These resulted in 99 reinstatement or re-engagement orders (0.3 per cent of the total) 1756 compensation orders, 210 redundancy payments, and 1234 cases where the tribunal left the parties to agree on the remedy. The median award of compensation was £1345. 119 applicants were awarded more than £5000.

These figures seem to prove conclusively that most dismissals are for good cause and that employers will escape liability accordingly. The number of successful claims will no doubt be further reduced as the 1985 requirement of two years' continuous service takes effect.

Chapter 4

Dismissal for Incapacity

4.01 Introduction

An employee's incapacity – i.e. his lack of capability or qualification for his work – is the first of the five grounds stated in section 57 of the Employment Protection (Consolidation) Act 1978 to justify his dismissal. The Act measures capacity by reference to 'skill, aptitude, health or any other physical or mental quality' and to qualifications – 'any degree, diploma, or other academic, technical or professional qualification relevant to the position the employee held'. There are then many different kinds of incapacity, ranging from incompetence when first appointed to illness or injury after years of able service. Such very different problems must be differently treated, as is clearly indicated by the ACAS Code of Practice and draft revision: Appendices 2 and 3.

4.02 Incompetence: warnings

We observe, to begin with, the practical difference between being unable to do a job properly and refusing to do it properly, or at all. The difference is important because of procedural requirements. Refusal is likely to be a question of misconduct, discussed in the next chapter, which as a general rule can be dealt with somewhat more rigorously than incapacity. An employee who is doing his best but still falls short of what is expected of him might sometimes expect guidance and support from his employer rather than final warnings and dismissal. His deficiencies may be due to circumstances beyond his control but within that of his employer, in which case dismissal would immediately appear unfair. So failure to make proper checks because of pressure of other work and with the background of a good work record was found not to justify dismissal in *Robertson* v. *Securicor* (1972), and adverse conditions of work – interruptions, noise and the like – which affected the employee's performance were taken into account also in *Hathaway* v. *F.W.D. Builders* (1975).

In any case a good working record deserves due recognition and if standards of work are criticised it must usually be right to give the employee the opportunity to improve his performance. In *Lumb* v. *Charcon Pipes* (1972), for example, a works manager of six years' excellent standing was dismissed by the new director because of the alleged high proportion of scrap in work for which he was responsible, and for abrasive relations with his subordinates, slow returns and generally carrying on as before under the new regime. The lack of warning was held unfair. A written complaint was not necessary, said the tribunal, but at least a frank talk might have helped the manager to change his ways. In *Tiptools* v. *Curtis* (1973) a grinder with twenty years' satisfactory service apart from a couple of current complaints about poor workmanship was given an important job to do. He did it badly and £30 worth of work had to be scrapped. Dismissal without 'serious personal warning' was likewise held unfair. The tribunal also suggested that if long-serving employees begin to find their work too hard employers should consider what other lighter work might be available.

What might therefore be called the normal response in incompetence cases was plainly stated by the National Industrial Relations Court, predecessor of the Employment Appeal Tribunal, in *James* v. *Waltham Holy Cross U.D.C.* (1973):

'An employer should be very slow to dismiss upon terms that an employee is incapable of performing the work he is employed to do without first telling [him] of the respects in which he is failing to do his job adequately, warning him of the possibility or likelihood of dismissal on this ground, and giving him an opportunity to improve his performance.'

On the other hand, of course, and other things being equal, there must be a limit to the incompetence employers have to tolerate. One mistake may be too many; the risks it indicates too great. This is particularly clear where health and safety are endangered, as illustrated in *Taylor* v. *Alidair* (1978) – a case of an airline pilot dismissed for landing an aeroplane badly and damaging it. This was an activity, said the Court of Appeal, 'in which the degree of professional skill which must be required is so high, and the potential consequences of the smallest departures from that high standard are so serious that one failure to perform in accordance with those standards is sufficient to justify dismissal'. Other similar instances cited were: 'the scientist operating nuclear reactors, the chemist in charge of research into the possible effects of, for example, thalidomide, the driver of the Manchester to London express, the driver of an articulated lorry full of sulphuric acid'. We shall see there may be other grounds again where warnings are not necessary, e.g. where it is clear they would be of no effect.

Further illustrations of acceptable and unacceptable levels of incompetence are given below, but one might conclude from those mentioned so far that wherever there is any reasonable doubt as to the proper course of action employers should err on the side of caution and advise their employees first as to the nature of their complaints and the consequences of failure to heed that advice.

4.03 Burden of proof of incompetence

The next preliminary point is as to how the employer is expected to prove his complaint. There are not always dramatic incidents like that in the case of *Taylor*, above, to point to, and in practice it is often very difficult to describe exactly how and why the employee's work is unsatisfactory. This difficulty need not be fatal. All that is needed, as we have said before, is an explanation of the employer's grievances amounting to a good *prima facie* case – not necessarily conclusive proof of each and every alleged shortcoming. To refer again to *Taylor*, Lord Denning said there that:

'Wherever a man is dismissed for incapacity or incompetence it is sufficient that the employer honestly believes on reasonable grounds that the man is incapable or incompetent. It is not necessary for the employer to prove that he is in fact incapable or incompetent.'

That is not to say that matters which can be proved need not be. And if facts or figures are produced it is open to the employee to give his own explanation or his own evidence to the contrary. In *Raynor* v. *Remploy* (1973), a branch manager was dismissed allegedly because of poor judgment and erratic administration. But he showed that he had inherited certain problems – 'His predecessor had committed suicide and morale in the group was low' – and he produced recent and improved trading figures. These effectively challenged his employer's assessment of his abilities and his dismissal was held unfair.

4.04　Trainees

We shall briefly consider now several examples of incompetence at various stages in working life, starting with training and examination requirements. There is a duty to 'maintain appraisals' on probationers and give such guidance as might be useful or fair – *P.O.* v *Mughal* (1977) – but otherwise the probationer has no special status or protection: *White* v. *London Transport Executive* (1981). If there are examinations to pass then failure to pass them justifies dismissal. Tribunals will not dispute professional requirements or professional assessments unless there is evidence of bias or other obvious unfairness. Their position in this respect was illustrated in a student nurse's case, *Witty* v. *Northamptonshire A.H.A.* (1976):

'There is one point which we think we must deal with in connection with the question: were the assessments right? The members of this tribunal are not medical men. We have insufficient knowledge to attempt to judge from our knowledge whether or not from the evidence which we have heard the applicant should have passed or failed the examination. What we have to decide is whether or not the assessors examined the applicant *bona fide* and exercising their professional judgment concluded that she had failed her exam in accordance with the standards in existence at the time. Furthermore, there is also the possibility that one examiner will look at a matter differently from another examiner. Although they might give different results it does not mean that one is "right" and the other "wrong" for this purpose. We accordingly have to decide whether or not the assessments were properly held in the sense that the assessors referred the applicant in the case of the second attempt and failed her in the final one in the sense of properly exercising their professional judgment.'

4.05 Professional standards

In another Health Service case, *Herdman Grant* v. *N.W. Surrey Health Authority* (1983), a very experienced and highly regarded nurse who had to give an injection was told by the sister and a colleague that there were 100 milligrams in a gram and not 1000 as she believed. She allowed her judgment to be overborne, and gave an injection of ten times the proper dose. On realising her mistake she told her employers, and fortunately no harm was done. Subsequently, however, she was given a final warning because of this incident, which left her sufficiently distracted that she misread a prescription sheet and administered a harmless antibiotic which had not been prescribed. In panic she then erased her initials from the prescription sheet, and then again voluntarily told her employers of what she had done. She was thereupon dismissed – but potentially serious though these incidents might have been, did they prove she was incapable? The tribunal held that in the light of her very high standing in the profession, of which it had every evidence, she was clearly not so. She had behaved as she did firstly because of the misjudgment of others and then as a result of what the tribunal regarded as an unjustified final warning. She was nonetheless partly at fault in allowing her judgment to be overborne and in falsifying the prescription sheet. Her claim therefore succeeded, but her compensation was reduced by 30 per cent.

Another N.H.S. case provides a contrast. In *Vega* v. *Tameside A.H.A.* (1980) the applicant was a health visitor. She was accused of 'over-reacting' in a particular case, and of being aggressive, rude and uncooperative in subsequent meetings. Following her suspension it was found that her case records, which had to be kept correctly and up to date for the sake of the patients and anyone else who might be called in urgently to see them, were in a 'chaotic state'. It appeared also that false entries of visits had been made. The combined effect of this evidence of *continuing unsuitability* was that the employing Authority had rightly seen her incapability as being of 'so serious and grave a nature that warning and retraining was not apposite and warranted summary dismissal'. Indeed, the E.A.T. held that the Authority would have been failing in its public duty not to have dismissed her.

Except for health and safety, therefore, employers generally may have to accept that 'everyone makes mistakes'. So dismissal of an industrial relations officer, whose recommendation to his employers not to recognise a union led to a strike and subsequent recognition of the union, was held to be unfair, partly because his recommendation had been accepted by more senior management: *Sherrard* v. *Tangye-Epco* (1975). The same conclusion was reached in *Hedges* v. *Phillips* (1975), where during the commotion of a change of premises a long-serving cashier made a slight clerical error which resulted in the firm being £3,500,000 overdrawn for one night and incurring thereby a loss of over £1000 in interest charges. In both cases compensation was reduced by half because of the employee's own share in the blame.

But once significant mistakes or other failings are pointed out, no great latitude can be expected. It may suddenly have become clear that the employee's temperament or attitude makes him simply the wrong man for the job. *O'Hagan* v. *Firestone Tyres* (1974) concerned an industrial relations officer whose job required 'an understanding of human nature, sensitivity to human problems and ability to inspire confidence', but whose arrogance and other defects of personality and manner obstructed union negotiations and alienated all around him. It was held that after several complaints to him about his conduct he was properly dismissed even though he had not been warned of possible dismissal. 'His incapability was irredeemable', said the tribunal.

Similarly, in *Spook* v. *Thackray* (1984) the employee was warned that his job would be in 'the severest of jeopardy' if his general approach to work did not 'quickly alter'. Twelve days later he failed to notify the company on the first day of absence through illness, as required by his contract. His dismissal was upheld as being 'within the band of reasonable responses of a reasonable employer' in the circumstances (though we might observe that warnings in such unspecific terms have sometimes been held inadequate).

4.06 Personality conflicts

One reason why an employee who has worked well in the past may now find himself subject to criticism is that of personality clashes with new colleagues or new supervisors. Such difficulties may be nobody's 'fault', but they can pose problems of unhappiness and obstructionism which should not be underestimated. It seems generally agreed in these cases that where no one can be blamed it will probably be the subordinate who has to give way – though not necessarily by dismissal. Dismissal will only be fair if every effort is made by management once it is or ought to be aware of the problem to resolve communication difficulties and improve the relationship, and if in the last resort the subordinate cannot be redeployed elsewhere: *Turner* v. *Vestric* (1980). If the employee is approaching retirement, dismissal will be a particularly severe penalty in these circumstances and thus probably unfair. Early retirement may be the preferable solution, as was stressed in *Norfolk* v. *Essex A.H.A.* (1975).

4.07 Promotion

Another hazard facing the employee is that of promotion beyond his abilities. If the employer dismisses within a relatively short time after promotion he is bound to be in some difficulty, having only just recognised and rewarded the employee's services, and being evidently at fault himself in misjudging the employee's potential. Great importance will be attached to the presence or absence of a training programme and to the length of the probationary period: *Bradley* v. *Opperman* (1975).

4.08 Managerial responsibilities

How far is it right to make supervisors 'carry the can' for their subordinates' failings? This recurrent issue was discussed in *Cockcroft* v. *Trendsetter Furniture* (1973), where a manager was dismissed without any personal warning, though there had been 'pep talks' in his department. The tribunal declared: 'It is no longer correct procedure to dismiss a departmental manager without any warning and without any adequate discussion of the problems confronting him merely because his department is open to criticism or because mistakes have occurred for which as departmental manager he is technically responsible'. This view was broadly supported in *Riley* v. *Frisby* (1982), in which a shop manageress was dismissed for refusing to make good the retail value of large stock deficiencies as required by her contract. Dismissal was held unfair on the basis that the requirement was unreasonable. It was pointed out that the loss could have occurred while she was on holiday, that she was held liable whether or not she was at fault, that the employer was claiming the retail value and not his actual loss, and that in the event she would be losing £20 a week from her take-home pay of £67. Conversely, if such losses could be attributed at least in part to a manager's failure to supervise effectively, dismissal would no doubt be upheld.

4.09   Ill health

How should employers respond when employees are incapacitated by genuine illness or injury? The problem arises very frequently but remains one of the most difficult and delicate in the whole area of personnel management.

There are many different aspects to be considered. Perhaps the first is that a serious illness or injury leading to lengthy absence from work does not of itself relieve the employer of the duty to decide what to do about it. We mentioned in Chapter 3 the law's reluctance to accept such circumstances as frustrating and thereby ending contracts of employment. Frustration remains a possible answer but should be regarded as unlikely in run-of-the-mill cases. The tribunals much prefer employers to make the kind of inquiries discussed below to bring the contract to an end. This clarifies the parties' positions, and may indeed be helpful to the employer in that he will usually find it easier to prove the day-to-day difficulties caused by the employee's absence than the long-term impossibility or impracticability of continued employment, which is what proof of frustration would require.

4.10 Procedures in illness cases

There are various sensible administrative precautions by which employers may seek to avoid some of the consequences of illness – such as requiring applicants for employment to undergo medical examinations or give undertakings as to their fitness for the work in question – but there are limits to what they can achieve. If the applicant appears fit, or in good faith says he is, he can scarcely be sacked because of his own or someone else's error of judgment. Deliberate concealment of one's disabilities should of course lead to a different answer, as in *O'Brien* v. *Prudential Assurance* (1979). The employee in this case had concealed a mental illness when he applied for his job. It was held that his illness was one which was capable of affecting his work, and dismissal justified accordingly. But we cannot say concealment always justifies dismissal. It might be unfair if, for example, the employee has given years of good service before his deception is discovered, or if it appears that the disability could not affect his work.

Another possible approach, as noted in [3.07], is to require the employee to sign a statement warning him that if he overstays his holidays for any reason, including illness, he will be held in breach of contract and dismissed. This precaution seems appropriate only for those who have histories of absenteeism but is nonetheless widely used. It seems that if the employee understands what he signs and there are no extenuating circumstances, dismissal for absence will be upheld.

We should note in particular that employers' responsibilities as regards dismissal for sickness are not determined by statutory or voluntary sick pay schemes. In *Hardwick* v. *Leeds A.H.A.* (1975) a nurse was dismissed for sickness absence as soon as the last day covered by her sick pay scheme had passed, in accordance with the

then existing practice of the National Health Service. The tribunal
found this arbitrary, impersonal and unfair. The converse position
is also worth mentioning, namely that employees cannot assume
that their contracts are bound to be continued at least until sick pay
rights expire. If it is clear immediately that the absentee will have to
be replaced, his employment may be ended at some earlier stage
even though sick pay continues.

It will be seen once more that each case must be treated on its
own merits and not by any rule of thumb. So in *Hardwick*, above,
the tribunal offered employers this practical advice, which they
would neglect at their peril:

> 'We do not wish to lay down any rigid procedures which we
> think should be followed but there seems here to have been lack
> of the personal contact which one normally finds in a personnel
> department. One wise thing which could be done in this type of
> situation would be to write to the employee (if somebody cannot
> call on her) about a fortnight before the sick pay is due to
> terminate and ask her if she can let the hospital know by letter or
> calling in for an interview what her present condition is in view
> of the fact that her sick pay is due to come to an end, and whether
> there is any likelihood of her returning to work in the near future
> as the hospital authority will have to consider the question of her
> future service. We certainly do not think that service should be
> terminated arbitrarily in this way.'

The two leading cases of *Egg Stores* v. *Leibovici* (1977) and *East
Lindsey D.C.* v. *Daubney* (1977) tell us there are in fact four or five
main lines of inquiry to which the tribunals expect convincing
answers from the employer. They will want to know, of course,
what is said to be the matter with the employee and how long he has
been away – but a lengthy absence by itself proves relatively little.
It may be more important to know what the prognosis is and when
he is thought likely to return. What difficulties does his absence
cause? Can a temporary appointment be made, or could existing
employees be expected temporarily to cover for him without undue
complaint – or is he a key figure whose absence inevitably creates
difficulties? In *Clark* v. *Coronel* (1972), for example, the frequent
absences of a small firm's only van driver were held sufficient to

justify dismissal. The firm had to be able to guarantee that collections and deliveries would be made when promised. As a general rule also, as indicated in *Hardwick*, employees must be kept posted as to developments at work affecting their future employment.

4.11 Burden of proof of illness

What evidence do employers, and hence tribunals, need as to the nature or genuineness of employees' illnesses, and their likely progress? Clearly sick notes must be provided, though that does not mean an employee can be dismissed for any and every failure to provide one – *Roustoby* v. *British Cocoa* (1973) – nor on the other hand that if a note *is* provided the employee is necessarily protected against dismissal, e.g. after being seen out enjoying himself when supposed to be sick in bed: *Hutchinson* v. *Enfield Mills* (1981). Employees cannot be expected to provide medical certificates guaranteeing future fitness, but employers may sometimes be justified in taking account of risks created by further likely illness: *Converfoam* v. *Bell* (1981). In that case, dismissal was upheld because another heart attack would have endangered fellow employees.

In certain exceptional situations, such as where ill-health affects long-serving employees in responsible positions, employers might find it necessary or desirable to seek independent medical advice, subject to the employee's consent. Where they receive conflicting advice it is for them to decide which to follow. If they act in good faith and dismiss as a result, that will not be held unfair merely because the advice turns out to be wrong and the employee proves fit for work.

While normally an employer will be guided by the reports of his employee's doctor or his own occupational health service, nonetheless the decisive factor may eventually be the rate of absenteeism or its effects upon the job. *Rolls-Royce* v. *Walpole* (1980) is a good example. In his last three years at work Mr Walpole was absent almost every other day. Nearly all his absences were duly certificated. He was counselled and warned against continued absenteeism, but to no effect. He claimed that his eventual dismissal was unfair because he could not be blamed for illness and because the employers had not asked for up-to-date medical reports either from his doctor or their own doctor. The Employment Appeal Tribunal said blameworthiness was only one factor among several. The overriding problem here was the scale of absenteeism, not its causes. In the circumstances, further medical information was unnecessary, and dismissal essentially a matter for the employers' discretion. One might add that dismissal at a very much earlier stage would no doubt have been equally acceptable to the tribunal. As another tribunal observed in *International Sports* v. *Thompson* (1980), after a fair review and appropriate warning an employer is always entitled to say: 'Enough is enough'.

A comparable case is *Harper* v. *National Coal Board* (1980). An employee's dismissal was upheld here because his epilepsy was thought to create risks for other employees – an almost unanswerable argument – even though his illness did not affect his ability to do his job and regardless of the medical officer's reluctance to recommend his retiral. The E.A.T. said that if the employer genuinely thought there were risks, that would be a 'substantial reason' for dismissal as provided by the Act, 'even where modern sophisticated opinion can be adduced to suggest that it has no scientific foundation'.

This latter comment is open to criticism, in that it seems to give free rein to uninformed personal prejudice. Such allegations have been made against employers in cases involving dismissal for mental illness and homosexuality, as to which the reader might consider *O'Brien* v. *Prudential Insurance* (1979) and *Saunders* v. *Scottish National Camps Association* (1981), in both of which dismissal was upheld. The difficulty cannot be denied. We recognise certain prejudices as so clearly harmful that they have to be regulated by law – notably as regards race, sex, union membership and spent convictions – and it may well be that there are others which should be similarly restrained. Until then, however, it is perhaps a little hard to say that because a person is an employer he must be free of the prejudices affecting nearly everyone else in our society. At the same time, of course, he is not obliged to act on others' fears or superstitions which he knows are groundless and which could be dispelled.

The case of *Seymour* v. *British Airways* (1983) tells us that the registered disabled have no special protection against dismissal for incapacity. The same is true even of those whose illness or injury is brought about by their employment. A case of interest here is *Hornby* v. *North Western R.H.A.* (1981), where an ambulanceman was disabled for life by fellow trade unionists for refusing to join a strike. The Authority tried to find him other work but none was acceptable, and eventually he had to be sacked because he could no longer do what he was paid to do. He argued that the Authority should somehow have supported him more strongly since he was acting on its behalf, but the tribunal held that there was nothing more the Authority could have done for him.

4.12 Consultation

We have mentioned the need to consult employees about the effects of their absence. Dismissing someone who is off sick without giving him any forewarning is almost always unfair. But if dismissal appears inevitable, as in *Walpole*, or perhaps because the rigours of the job demand a very high standard of fitness and dependability, then nothing the employee could say would affect the position and so it would be pointless to insist on consultation, as was accepted in *Taylorplan* v. *McInally* (1980) and *Leonard* v. *Fergus* (1979). But cases such as these, where consultation was held to be unnecessary, should be regarded as exceptions to the general rule.

The overall position, then, is that a significant degree of incapacity or absenteeism must ultimately justify dismissal. Employers do not owe their employees a living indefinitely. They must nonetheless show the compassion due to those who have given years of service, and who may now face hardship and unhappiness through no fault of their own.

4.13 Alternative employment

In particular, the employer owes it to employees who can no longer do the work they were taken on to do to try to find them alternative employment, usually of a lighter nature and possibly at a lower rate of pay. He is not, however, obliged to create jobs for them which did not previously exist: *M.A.N.W.E.B.* v. *Taylor* (1975). Tribunals have also suggested that when illness makes dismissal unavoidable, employers might put employees in 'holding' or 'suspense departments', undertaking to give them priority for any suitable vacancy which might arise if and when they are fit to return. This would be a commitment made in the interests of recovery and good industrial relations but it would not appear legally enforceable.

Chapter 5

Misconduct, Illegality and Other Substantial Reasons for Dismissal

5.01 Misconduct

Misconduct, the second ground for dismissal recognised by the Employment Protection (Consolidation) Act, covers a multitude of sins. What is at stake is whether the employee's conduct, deliberate or inadvertent, at work or away from it, conflicts significantly with his duties to his employer. There are countless cases on every conceivable and inconceivable form of misconduct, but we shall confine ourselves here to a representative selection under the broad headings of disobedience, insolence, carelessness, absenteeism (including strike action), criminal conduct and 'miscellaneous'. Related questions of investigation of alleged offences, warnings and other procedural aspects are enlarged upon in Chapter 6. It will be appreciated that all the cases mentioned are examples, not rules. They indicate how tribunals are likely to respond to similar situations, but do not determine the outcome. Each case turns very much on its own facts.

5.02 Disobedience

An employer seeking to dismiss for disobedience must establish first of all that the order which he says was disobeyed was a lawful and reasonable one. Orders are lawful and reasonable if and insofar as they are within the terms of the contract of employment – and hence the importance of written job descriptions, as urged in

Chapter 1 – but, of course, employers sometimes over-reach themselves in the terms they impose. The courts will not enforce contracts designed to evade payment of tax or which impose, for example, 'obviously and intolerably unfair' requirements upon employees, as with the arbitrary grading system in *Payne* v. *Spook* (1984). Unreasonable exploitation cases apart, however, once we know what the employee's job is we can say with some certainty that wilful refusal to do it must justify dismissal. But that does not necessarily mean dismissal on the spot, if only because some aspects of the employee's duties are less important than others, and also because it is usually helpful to allow time for clarification or second thoughts.

Miscellaneous examples of disobedience include *Lambsdale* v. *H.M.S.O.* (1975), which involved an industrial relations manager's refusal to attend a company meeting to discuss his policies; *Oxley* v. *East Berkshire H.A.* (1983), in which a nurse refused to treat patients; *Riley* v. *Kirklees A.H.A.* (1977), involving a hospital porter's refusal to empty bins; *Atkin* v. *Enfield Hospital* (1975), concerning a nurse's refusal to wear correct uniform. Dismissal after due warning was upheld in each case. An observation from *Riley's* case may be of interest:

'It is not uncommon for this tribunal to hear an employee taking a stand on what he describes as "a principle", but it often turns out to be more a matter of obstinacy on his part rather than a genuine principle. We are of the view that this was the position here ... It would put employers in an impossible position if, without any very compelling reason, employees could suddenly refuse to do a job which is part of their contract of employment and which they have done before, and then expect to continue in their employment ... It was open to the applicant to have raised this matter as a grievance with his employers if he had so wished.'

Where an employee refused to sign a written statement of terms of employment (when signature is not required by law but may be by works rule) this was regarded as breach of a minor term of the contract which initially at least did not warrant dismissal and should have been dealt with by a warning: *Turner* v. *Yates* (1972).

In *Young* v. *Thomas* (1972), an employee was dismissed for private use of his employer's vehicles which he knew was prohibited. This was unfair because in the past the company had seemed to condone private use, had not made it clear that the penalty was dismissal, and had taken insufficient account of thirty-two years' loyal service. But his compensation was cut by half because he knew the practice was forbidden. Refusal to work overtime does not justify dismissal if overtime is optional, nor does a request to do it justify resignation. Concerted refusal may be a form of industrial action: see [5.10]. Dismissal for first offences of smoking or drinking in breach of works rules would probably be treated in the same way, unless there were some obvious danger, or, as regards drinking, further objectionable behaviour: *Trusthouse* v. *Adonis* (1984); *Brooks* v. *Skinner* (1984).

So far as enforcement of safety rules in particular is concerned, dismissal seems very much a measure of last resort. It gets rid of somebody who breaks the rules, but does not ensure that those still at work observe them. Cooperation in this of all contexts is obviously preferable to compulsion. The fact remains that employers are exposed to prosecution or liability in damages if precautions are not taken, and dismissal may become inevitable. Defiance of safety rules justified dismissal in *Taylor* v. *Bowater* (1973), but not in *Mayhew* v. *Anderson* (1978) where the safety equipment was not suitable for the particular employee.

Employers can usually assume that employees know of and are bound by agreements made with their unions. So when his union agreed that certain safety precautions were necessary, the employee who refused to take them was held fairly dismissed in *Lindsay* v. *Dunlop* (1980). But the employee will probably get the benefit of the doubt if it is not clear he knew of the agreement or for some other good reason should not be bound by it. In *Brooks* v. *Skinner*, the case cited above, management and union agreed that employees who over-indulged at the company's Christmas party and were absent from work as a result could be instantly dismissed. Mr Brooks was then dismissed on these grounds, but won his claim because the agreement had not been put to him in writing and so he did not know he would be dismissed if he did not return to work.

5.03   Interpretation of terms

Differences of opinions as to the meaning of the terms in a contract may lead to disputes and dismissals. An employer might, for example, tell an employee to do something he has not done before, or to do his job in a different way, which the employer says is part of the contract but which the employee regards as a completely new burden and one he is not obliged to accept. It is then a question of trying to interpret what has been agreed in a just, sensible and practical way.

Glitz v. *Watford Electric* (1979) is a straightforward example. A girl was taken on in a small office as 'copy typist/general clerical duties clerk'. No mention was made of use of the office duplicator, and it was not until some three years later that she was first told to use it. She refused on health grounds. It was held that use of the duplicator was part and parcel of 'general clerical duties', even though not previously required of her. The fact that the smell made her feel ill was unfortunate, but it did not affect anyone else and the end result was that she could not or would not do what she was employed to do. She was therefore fairly dismissed.

Huxtable v. *Devon A.H.A.* (1975) is a comparable case. A woman was employed here as a 'nurse auxiliary'. For the following three years she worked exclusively on the hospital's maternity ward. She was then instructed to move to the geriatric ward; she refused and was fired. Her argument was that as nurse auxiliary in the maternity ward, which was what she said she had become, she could not lawfully be required to work elsewhere in the hospital. The tribunal said that mobility was inherent in her job title and that it would be impossible to run a hospital if employees could not be moved from one ward to another just because they happened to have worked in one for some months or years. She was therefore fairly dismissed.

In contrast is *Redbridge L.B.C.* v. *Fishman* (1978). A person employed as 'director of visual resources' at a college agreed to give twelve hours a week English teaching. At a later date she was ordered to give eighteen hours. She declined, and was dismissed. She won her case because eighteen hours' teaching was virtually a full-time English teacher's job, and that was not what she was taken on to do.

The message from these three cases – and many others like them – is reasonably clear and most important. The fact that a job has been done in a particular way or in a particular place does not of itself mean that the way or place is of the essence of the job and cannot be altered, or has to be negotiated. Some degree of mobility or adaptability is a prerequisite of every employment. But, at least in theory, that does not entitle the employer to make the employee do a different job altogether. There are always problems of drawing the line, some of which we have touched on already in [1.10] and [3.10], and which we discuss below in [5.05] and in [7.4] and [7.7].

Assuming for a moment that there is no dispute about the meaning of any particular contractual commitment, we might observe in passing that a literal or excessive observance of it (by either side) is as likely to be objectionable as disregarding it entirely. An example is *Evans* v. *Gwent H.A.* (1983), where an ambulanceman due to end his shift at 4 pm found himself still burdened with patients at that time and so left them in the vehicle at the ambulance station for someone else to take home. With a record of unsatisfactory behaviour his dismissal for this incident was upheld, and the tribunal rejected the union view that his 'right' to finish at 4 pm was a major issue of principle. He would in any case have been paid incidental overtime. The consequences of 'working to rule' as a form of industrial action are considered below: [5.10].

The contractual duty which the employee is alleged to have broken need not be expressly stated in his contract. It may be read in as reasonably incidental to terms expressly agreed, or added as an implied term by the law, as explained in Chapter 1 and pursued immediately below. As regards matters reasonably incidental to the contract, several cases tell us that employees are obliged to conform to reasonable norms of behaviour and dress demanded by their employers. In various formal situations, for example, women may be required to wear dresses rather than trouser suits or slacks. Wearing badges announcing one's sexual proclivities may be objectionable to customers or other employees, as may 'affairs' within the office: *Boychuk* v. *Simmons* (1977); *Newman* v. *Alarmco* (1976). On the other hand, an employee who disobeyed an order to have his hair cut was held unfairly dismissed in *O'Connor* v. *MacPherson* (1974), where the employer's preference was evidently of a personal or aesthetic nature and not justifiable by reference to safety or hygiene or public relations requirements.

5.04   Implied terms

We saw in Chapter 1 the wide effect of the duties of obedience, care, competence and good faith which are implied by law. One particular issue we might usefully mention again here is that of spare time activities. We noted that spare time work might be forbidden if it involved competition with or other detriment to one's own employer. Many other spare time activities are also affected, contrary to the popular misconception that what a person does in his spare time is his own business. A serious breach of the law or other objectionable behaviour in any context may well damage the employer's reputation or suggest unfitness for office. *Margerison* v. *Yorkshire R.H.A.* (1976) is a convincing example. The case concerned an ambulanceman who returned after hours to pester the daughter of a patient he had taken to hospital earlier that day, who was left alone in the house. He made his way in on a pretext, kissed the girl against her will and knowing he was not welcome called again a few days later to take her to the cinema. He was held fairly dismissed for gross abuse of trust.

The conduct complained of must, of course, have some relevance to the job in hand. In *Thompson* v. *Alloa Motors* (1983) the applicant, a petrol pump attendant, accidentally drove into a pump as she was leaving work and caused considerable damage. She was learning to drive and was properly accompanied. Her dismissal was unfair because the accident did not affect her ability to do her work, was not likely to be repeated, and was not in any case sufficient to justify dismissal.

5.05   Changing the terms

We return now to the vexed question of employers' powers unilaterally to change the terms of their contracts, as explored earlier in [1.10] and [3.10]. Contracts of employment may last for many years. The nature of the job in hand and the circumstances in which it is done necessarily change and develop during that time.

No one could reasonably insist that the precise terms on which he began work should remain for ever sacrosanct. The unions themselves, as we have remarked before, claim the power to alter the terms when they demand more pay or shorter hours, or seek to impose a closed shop agreement where none previously existed. The problem is as always that of defining and limiting the rights involved.

From the employer's point of view at least, difficulties may be largely overcome if the contract expressly provides for change, as many do. Changes in occupation, status or place of work are all equally feasible if so provided – as, for example, the contractual right to move an export sales engineer to home sales in *Deeley* v. *B.R.E.* (1980), or business manager to customer liaison officer under a clause stating: 'Should the interest of the company demand it ... the particular nature of your job may be changed' in *Bex* v. *Securicor* (1972). If the contract expressly or even impliedly requires mobility, refusal to move justifies dismissal. Workers in building and other contracting jobs are among those subject to implied obligations to move, but usually (depending on the nature of the enterprise) only to sites within reasonable commuting distance of home: *Jones* v. *Associated Tunnelling* (1981). Greater mobility may be expected at managerial level: *Little* v. *Charterhouse* (1980).

Without the express or implied authority of the contract, however, management's position becomes more complicated. Employers may sometimes be able to compel acceptance of new terms, effectively involving breach of the old ones, if there are 'sound business reasons' for them. The courts understand that if employers cannot respond to economic pressures they will go out of business, which does not usually benefit anybody. In *Chubb* v. *Harper* (1983), for example, the company reorganised because of declining sales and offered a sales representative a new contract in a new area. He rejected it because he feared a considerable drop in earnings and because he did not know the area. He was then dismissed for refusing to accept these changes. The tribunal agreed that his response was reasonable, but that of itself did not make his employer's demand unreasonable. It was necessary to examine the advantages of reorganisation and consider whether the company had acted reasonably in offering new contracts and in deciding that the advantages to them outweighed the disadvantages to the employee. He lost his claim accordingly.

There may be no alternative, then, but to change hours, reduce overtime, or alter holiday arrangements. Such changes may have serious consequences for the employee, but without redress if he cannot or will not accept them. A leading case is *Banerjee* v. *City A.H.A.* (1979), where the employer decided to replace two part-time consultants by one full-timer. Mr Banerjee, one of the part-timers, thus lost his job through no fault of his own but because the employer had changed the specifications. He had no claim for redundancy pay, since the overall need for consultants was not affected, and as a matter of principle would have had no claim for compensation for unfair dismissal either because, as the tribunal recognised, employers had to be free to decide their own staffing requirements. In the event he won his case, but really only on a technicality – that the Authority did not produce any sufficient evidence to explain their new policy. This was an omission which employers could easily rectify in future cases.

These cases may be contrasted with others such as *Spencer-Jones* v. *Timmens Moreland* (1974), where a hairdresser was held unfairly dismissed for refusing to work on Saturday afternoons. This extension of her hours was seen as a matter of employer's preference rather than 'market forces', but in the light of more recent cases should perhaps be regarded as a borderline case. Cutting an hourly rate without the employee's agreement was held to be a blameworthy breach in *Scott* v. *Formica* (1975), as was ordering men to work five machines instead of four – imposing without consultation a 20 per cent increase in workload – in *Worsnip* v. *Hawke* (1975). In *McNeil* v. *Crimin* (1984) the employer was not satisfied with a foreman electrician's perform-ance of his duties and so ordered him to work temporarily under the supervision of an ordinary electrician. This was held to be a repudiatory breach of contract by the employer which justified the foreman's claim for compensation for constructive dismissal.

All the cases just mentioned concern dismissals arising out of refusal to accept change. If the employee stays at work, the change is thus apparently made binding upon him, and a different situation arises. *Burdett Coutts* v. *Hertfordshire C.C.* (1984) is a case in point. The local authority had to economise because of cuts in government grants, and so substantially reduced the pay and hours of certain school dinner ladies. Those who refused to accept the new terms remained at work but sued for damages for breach of contract. Their claims were upheld in the High Court, on the basis that such fundamental changes constituted a repudiatory breach. The fact that the employees remained at work did not stop them claiming, since they did so under protest. This conclusion seems to contradict the view advanced earlier that changes resulting from economic pressures must be accepted, even where they involve breach of contract. But we see from *Kent C.C.* v. *Gilham* (1985), a similar case, that the proper course of action for the employer in these circumstances is to end the old contract and offer a new one. The Court of Appeal indicated in *Gilham* that if the new contract was a realistic alternative to unemployment, anyone dismissed for rejecting it would probably lose his or her claim for compensation (even though this particular employer was held to have acted unreasonably in disregarding a national agreement on conditions of employment).

5.06 Consultation

What, if any, obligations are employers under to consult employees beforehand about the kind of changes we have been discussing? The ACAS Code (see Appendix 2 and draft revised edition in Appendix 3) naturally advises consultation on every issue of substance, but while the law recognises consultation as desirable it stops short of insistence. This was the decision of the Court of Appeal in *Hollister* v. *N.F.U.* (1979), where new terms were held binding despite lack of consultation. The reason is that after all possible consultations have taken place, employees may still not agree with what is proposed, but their disagreement would not and could not affect the business pressures upon the employer which led to the proposals and which are as we have said good grounds for introducing changes. That is not to say that consultation and procedural propriety generally are not important. Apart from the damage done to good industrial relations, failure to discuss in advance of decisions may always lead to the kind of avoidable misunderstanding or *impasse* which can in turn make dismissal unfair. And conversely, if the union accepts change, the position of the individual objector is weakened accordingly: see [5.02].

5.07   Insolence

Just as gross offensiveness by an employer may justify an employee's claim for constructive dismissal (see [3.09]), so insults or obvious contempt for one's employer (as distinct of course from mere disagreement or criticism) may justify dismissal. Where a manager told a cleaner three times to do a job and was in return enjoined to 'fuck off', the cleaner's dismissal was upheld by the tribunal: *Walters* v. *Top Crust* (1972). On the other hand, when an apprentice told the manager who had reprimanded him: 'You couldn't have done any fucking better', this view, however uncharitable, was held not to warrant dismissal. It was an isolated incident, and in any case employers were still to some extent *in loco parentis* and as such apparently obliged to tolerate a certain amount of 'lip'. A warning or suspension was said to be the proper response in this case.

No great importance should necessarily be attached to things said in the heat of the moment. 'We do not think one rude comment made in a moment of stress after five years of good work was serious enough to merit instant dismissal': *Rosenthall* v. *Butler* (1972). But compensation might well be reduced, particularly if the employee refuses to apologise. As between employees at much the same level, rudeness may be of little significance. In *King* v. *Motorway Tyres* (1975), for example, it was held unfair to dismiss a service manager for telling his branch manager to 'fuck off'. A severe reprimand and final warning were thought to be more appropriate. But rudeness or complaints of rudeness to customers will usually justify dismissal, even if the incidents cannot all be substantiated.

5.08   Carelessness

It may be difficult to draw a dividing line between carelessness and incompetence, but sometimes necessary to do so. Problems of incompetence are the more likely to require counselling and warning, as we saw in Chapter 4. But if an employee shows he 'couldn't care less' about his work, dismissal is usually appropriate. Standing by and allowing a defective machine to produce scrap justified dismissal in *Comerford* v. *Swel Foods* (1972) – the more clearly so because the employee was a foreman. In *McPhie* v. *Wimpey* (1981) two fitters signed a vehicle service form. Ten days later the gear box seized up. Apart from the damage to the vehicle there was the risk of an accident and of the employer's loss of his licence. On the balance of probabilities the gear box seized up because it had not been serviced. It was not known which employee was responsible but both had signed. Both were then to blame, and in view of the seriousness of the matter, both were held to have been fairly dismissed.

If an employer seems to condone poor standards, then dismissal without previous warning will probably be unfair. So in *Ayub* v. *Vauxhall* (1978) an employee's dismissal on being found asleep on the night shift after finishing his quota was held unfair because management had previously tolerated this practice. And as we have mentioned before, management must take into account adverse working conditions which affect performance.

5.09 Absenteeism

Generally speaking, misconduct in the form of poor time-keeping does not warrant dismissal without evidence of a record in that respect, accompanied by suitable warnings. Employers must beware of taking a person's job from him because he has lost a few minutes here or there. But even so, dismissal might be justified for a single absence if the employee knows he is specially needed at that particular time, or if his absence involves falsifying clocking on or off times: *Stewart* v. *Western S.M.T.* (1978). The problem of employees overstaying their leave by a day or two or three may be dealt with by requiring them to sign statements beforehand acknowledging termination of their contracts in that event: see [3.7].

5.10 Strikes and other 'industrial action'

Absence from work because of strike action calls for separate treatment. What we say about strikes applies equally to other forms of industrial action (or inaction, as it might more accurately be called), such as working to rule, going slow, 'working without enthusiasm', overtime bans – whether or not overtime is voluntary: *Power Packing* v. *Faust* (1983) – and the like, if and insofar as they involve concerted breaches of contracts of employment. Threatening such action does not amount to breach.

Employees sometimes find it difficult to see how working to rule can be regarded as a breach of contract, but even on the assumption that the rule in question is laid down by the employer – and often enough it turns out to have been devised on the shop floor – the answer is reasonably clear. In the past the rule will have been observed in a way acceptable to both sides. From the time the work to rule begins it is observed in a quite different way and without agreement. One must then ask what brought about the new interpretation. The answer will be that it is intended to bring the work to a standstill and so put pressure upon the employer. On the face of it that must be a breach of contract. The issue was explored at length and this same conclusion reached in *Secretary of State* v. *A.S.L.E.F.* (1972), where in the course of an industrial dispute railwaymen applied safety rules in such a way as to cause chaos.

The question, then, is whether or when an employer can dismiss employees for going on strike. In effect we are considering what if anything is meant by the expression 'the right to strike', which is so widely and frequently invoked. In attempting briefly to provide an answer to this fundamental question, we should note first the rules most directly affecting unions – those on liability for inducing a breach of contract. Basically the position is that if A knows that B and C have a contract and he deliberately interferes with this relationship, he can be liable in damages to either or both of them for the common law 'tort' or civil wrong of inducing a breach of contract. But if that inducement takes place 'in contemplation or furtherance of a trade dispute', section 13 of the Trade Union and Labour Relations Act 1974, as amended by the Employment Acts 1980–2 and Trade Union Act 1984, says that liability in tort does not arise. Unions (or unofficial organisations – the law does not distinguish between them, perhaps to the unions' detriment) can therefore call out their members in breach of their contracts of employment without incurring any liability so long as there is a trade dispute in prospect and subject to the balloting requirements of the 1984 Act and the limitations on secondary action imposed in 1980. Trade disputes are defined in section 29 of the 1974 Act essentially as matters concerning one's own conditions of employment – and excluding therefore inter union disputes, political strikes and other extraneous issues.

The individual employee who responds to the call and stops work or refuses to cross a picket line must almost always be in breach of contract in so doing. This is quite clear when he stops work without giving notice, and may be so even when he does give notice. The reason is that the purpose of notice is to end the contract and not to suspend it, and so misusing provisions as to notice might well amount to breach. Only where the employee is actually prevented from working by circumstances beyond his control – for example, by falling ill, or when the employer breaks his side of the contract by giving unlawful orders, for instance, or allowing conditions of work to become too dangerous or otherwise intolerable – could a 'downer' be legally justified. The usual legal remedy for any breach of contract is, of course, a claim for damages, but in employment the simplest solution for the employer is not to pay for work which has not been done. Alternatively he may wish to consider dismissal.

His rights in this event depend first of all on whether he dismisses during or after the strike. Section 62 of the Employment Protection (Consolidation) Act 1978 expressly permits dismissal of employees *while they are on strike* or taking other concerted industrial action to enforce demands. The tribunals are not allowed to take sides here. It does not matter whether the strike was official or unofficial, spurious, provoked or entirely justified. But the rule is perhaps less remarkable than it appears because it applies only where there is no victimisation. Effectively, therefore, all the strikers may be dismissed or none at all, unless there is some reason unrelated to the strike which justifies dismissal of a particular individual or refusal to re-employ him. Former employees may, however, be selectively re-employed not less than three months after their dismissal. This right to dismiss everyone is of its nature hardly ever exercised, but is a recognition that in the last resort an employer may need to break the deadlock to save his business and should be free to start again with new staff.

The more controversial issue concerns the rights of the parties once the strike is over and everyone is back at work. Can the employer then 'pick off' individual employees? The answer is that he can, but only if he can show they were dismissed because of unacceptable breaches of contract – high levels of absenteeism or misconduct or whatever – and not by way of victimisation.

Fleming and Dickens v. *Ealing A.H.A.*(1980) is a useful illustration. These two gentlemen were electrical maintenance workers at a hospital and members of the Amalgamated Union of Engineering Workers. They and others were engaged in a so-called work to rule whose effect was directly to endanger patients and which was in breach of a collective agreement. With patients' lives and health at risk the tribunal found Mr Fleming's attitude and behaviour 'frankly horrifying', and added that it 'could not see how management could face future problems with any feeling of confidence knowing that among its tradesmen was a union shop steward who might at any point decline some essential instruction on some novel or ... specious ground'. So what legal right did Mr Fleming have to do as he did, and what should management's response have been?

The tribunal flatly rejected Mr Fleming's 'assumption that once one had declared a state of "industrial action" one's legal obligations were suspended and one could act as one liked'. This crucial passage followed:

> 'We know of no provision whereby an employee under the industrial law of this country is exempted from a breach of his own contract merely because he declares a state of "industrial action".'

Both applicants had not only broken their contracts but had wilfully and without warning or justification refused an order affecting the health and safety of others dependent upon them. The tribunal agreed that their dismissals for misconduct were therefore 'fully justified'.

This case – and many more besides – clearly supports two basic propositions: first the point made earlier that a strike or other industrial action is almost always in breach of contract, and second that some breaches of contract justify dismissal. Confirmation comes from the ruling of the Employment Appeal Tribunal in *Simmonds* v. *Hoover* (1975):

'Here there was a settled, confirmed and continued intention on the part of the employee not to do any of the work which under his contract he had engaged to do; which was the whole purpose of the contract. Judged by the usual standards, such conduct by the employee appears to us to be repudiatory of the contract of employment. We should not be taken to be saying that all strikes are necessarily repudiatory, though usually they will be. For example, it could hardly be said that a strike of employees in opposition to demands by an employer in breach of contract by him would be repudiatory. But what might be called a 'real' strike in our judgment always will be.'

5.11 Organiser or participant?

It seems then that one is free to withdraw one's labour and run the risk of being sacked for so doing – which could hardly be described as a 'right'. But that is not the whole story. There is a right to strike, but it is to be found in the rule we began with – section 13 of the Trade Union and Labour Relations Act – and not in the terms on which individuals are employed. It will be recalled that section 13 grants immunity from liability in tort to anyone who induces a breach of contract in contemplation or furtherance of a trade dispute (subject to balloting requirements and the protection given by section 17 of the Employment Act 1980 to wholly uninvolved and independent employers). In effect, a distinction is drawn between those who organise strikes or other forms of industrial action – official or otherwise – and those who actually take part in them. The Act grants immunity to the organisers in disputes against their own employers – an essential safeguard for unions, at least – but neither this nor any other law relieves individual employees of the consequences of breaking their own contracts. And if any organiser is also a participant in a strike he risks dismissal for breach of contract just like anyone else.

5.12 Shop stewards

The same line of argument applies specifically to shop stewards.

Union officials are bound to disagree with management sooner or later and must be free to advise their members accordingly. No question of dismissal on these grounds alone could arise, and indeed it is forbidden by section 58 of the 1978 Act. On the other hand, when management and labour make an agreement, both sides are morally obliged to carry it out. Shop stewards who disregard their responsibilites in this respect undoubtedly risk dismissal. In *McQuade* v. *Scotbeef* (1975), for example, a steward's dismissal was upheld for repeatedly flouting agreed disputes procedure.

Whether in practice an employer would be wise to exercise his undoubted legal rights is of course another matter, depending very much on the likely reactions of his other employees.

5.13   Criminal offences

An employee who commits a criminal offence does not automatically forfeit his job, as the ACAS Code points out, but if the crime is of any real consequence, he necessarily puts it at risk. The same is true if he is reasonably believed to have committed such an offence. (We pursue the vexed problem of proof in [6.02].) The offence need not be committed at work nor have any direct connection with it. It is sufficient if its effect is to make the employee a bad risk at work, or to damage his employer's reputation or be unacceptable to fellow employees. Employees sometimes argue that they are thereby punished twice, and that that is unfair. The argument is patently wrong, since employers have interests to protect which are clearly separate from the state's, and which need a different kind of protection.

Very trivial offences or those having no effect whatever on employment, however, do not justify dismissal. The question is, as before, whether dismissal would be within the band of reasonable responses. Much depends, therefore, on the nature of the crime and the nature of the job. Blanket conditions of employment requiring or permitting dismissal for any breach of the law are self-evidently unjust. It is most important that the rules should give employers discretion as to how to treat trivial or otherwise excusable offences.

We can say with reasonable certainty that almost any theft at work, of all but the most trivial nature, will be ground for dismissal, and that thefts in any other context may well be equally seriously regarded. Three Health Service cases provide helpful illustrations. The applicant in *Brown* v. *S.E.Hampshire H.A.* (1983) was a hospital kitchen superintendent with a good work record. He was dismissed for theft of 50 pence worth of vegetables. The tribunal noted that two other employees had been caught eating hospital food and although required to pay for it were only warned and not dismissed, but the tribunal believed Mr Brown's position was different. He had deliberately removed the food and hidden it, not simply eaten a little while on duty, and in any case he occupied a post of responsibility and trust. His dismissal was upheld. Similarly, in *Dykyj* v. *Barnet A.H.A.* (1981) a mental hospital nurse was held rightly dismissed for the alleged theft of a packet of cigarettes from a patient – which very well illustrates how easily relationships of trust may be destroyed and the severe consequences which are bound to follow.

In *Shan* v. *Croydon A.H.A.* (1975) the applicant was a doctor. She was charged with stealing a handbag worth £3 from a shop. She denied the charge but was convicted and fined £50. Her dismissal likewise was upheld. Her offence – which for practical purposes was proved by her conviction, despite her denials – was not committed at work but nonetheless revealed her as a bad risk in a context where opportunities for abuse of trust were unlimited and their consequences potentially extremely damaging.

Exceptional cases of thefts brought about by nervous breakdowns, overwhelming domestic pressures and the like might properly be more leniently treated – for example, by transfer to some less responsible post.

Fighting and assaults represent another very common problem area. Normally dismissal is appropriate, preferably on the basis of a clear rule to that effect. But as with thefts we cannot say that all such incidents in all circumstances should be dealt with in this way. A distinction must be drawn, for example, between bullying and a punch or push in self-defence or under gross provocation. A minor 'scrap' which hurts no one might perhaps be treated quite leniently. In *Meyer* v. *Rogers* (1978) dismissal for fighting was held unfair because of lack of clarity in the rules, no particular danger but some element of provocation and failure to consider penalties short of dismissal. But the employee lost 10 per cent of his compensation because of his own fault in the matter. If it is impossible to find who is at fault in a serious incident it may still be wrong to sack both parties involved. One man may have a record of misconduct; the other not. The latter should be given credit for his good character: *Sherrier* v. *Ford* (1976). On the other hand, even a 'technical' assault upon a senior officer – by molesting or threatening him or her – will very probably justify dismissal: *Harvey* v. *National Heart and Chest Hospitals* (1983).

Assorted other offences are illustrated in *Nottinghamshire C.C.* v. *Bowly* (1978), where a teacher was held fairly dismissed for gross indecency; *Norfolk C.C.* v. *Bernard* (1979), where an advisory drama teacher was found unfairly dismissed for cultivating cannabis (a doubtful decision): *Bradshaw* v. *Rugby Portland* (1972), where dismissal following a conviction and minor penalty for incest was held unfair in the case of a labourer whose work did not bring him into contact with women.

5.14   Procedures

Assuming that the offence justifies dismissal, employers are free to dismiss employees caught red-handed or against whom investigation shows there are 'solid, sensible grounds for suspicion' without having to wait for the police to prosecute, or still less for conviction: *Harris* v. *Courage* (1982). An employer cannot be expected to do more than act fairly in the light of information reasonably available to him at the time of dismissal. It follows that a subsequent acquittal does not in any way prove dismissal unfair (just as after-acquired information cannot make fair a dismissal which would otherwise be unjustified). If the employer prefers to await the outcome of criminal proceedings he would probably be wiser to suspend the employee on full pay in the meantime. Investigations should be undertaken promptly and every opportunity given to the employee to state his case – unless guilt is obvious or admitted.

Failure to disclose previous convictions may justify dismissal from a position of trust, unless the employee is protected by the Rehabilitation of Offenders Act 1974: see [3.5]. In *Torr* v. *B.R.Board* (1977) it was discovered that the employee had lied at interview when asked about previous convictions. His conviction was not 'spent' as provided by the Act, and his dismissal was upheld accordingly. The Employment Appeal Tribunal said that employers were not obliged to adopt the philosophy of the Act in circumstances to which it did not apply.

5.15 Miscellaneous

A wide variety of other wrongs which have been regarded as misconduct serious enough to justify dismissal include poor record keeping, refusal to attend courses, breach of confidentiality, and setting oneself up in competition with one's employers. This latter ground is illustrated in *Golden Cross* v. *Lovell* (1979). A company warehouse manager had assisted a former employee, now a potential competitor of the company, by painting and repairing his vehicles on company premises. His disloyalty and lying about his actions when challenged were held to make his dismissal fair. See also 'Other substantial reasons', below [5.17].

5.16 Illegality

Another statutory ground for dismissal is that continued employment would involve employer or employee in breaking some statutory duty or restriction. Typical examples are where employees are taken on as drivers but lose their licences, or where they fail to meet examination or other standards of proficiency laid down by statute, or cannot obtain work permits. In the former cases, however, dismissal might still be unfair if alternative arrangements are feasible, as in *Sutcliffe* v. *Pinney* (1977), where it was held that the employee should have been given more time to take his examinations. One must be sure also that the law in question does apply to the particular case since dismissal under a mistaken impression of its effect could be unfair.

5.17 Other substantial reasons

An employer who cannot prove his employee's incapacity or

misconduct, or that continued employment would be illegal, and who does not dismiss because of redundancy (which we consider separately in Chapter 7), will nonetheless escape liability on showing 'some other substantial reason of a kind such as to justify the dismissal of an employee holding the position which that employee held', as section 57 (1) of the 1978 Act puts it. To be on the safe side, employers might wish to allege both misconduct (or other specific ground) *and* other substantial reason.

This is obviously a hold-all provision, whose application turns very much on the nature of the employment in question. So, as the Court of Appeal said in *Dobie* v. *Burns* (1984), different types of reasons could justify dismissal of the office boy from those which could justify dismissal of the managing director. The Employment Appeal Tribunal has said that a substantial reason is one which is not 'whimsical or capricious ... which no person of ordinary sense would entertain', but one which that employer genuinely believes to be fair, and which most employers could be expected so to believe – even though it might in fact be ill-founded.

Such very wide phraseology, wavering uncertainly between the subjective opinion of the employer in the case and the need for some kind of objective assessment of 'substantiality', may leave employees with relatively little protection. We have seen that employers can call in aid 'sound, good business reasons' or simply reasons which have 'discernible advantages to the organisation' – *Hollister* v. *N.F.U.* (1979); *Bowater* v. *McCormack* (1980) – to support unilateral and fundamental changes in conditions of employment, short of redundancy, which employees must accept or else leave without redress (see *Genower* v. *Ealing A.H.A.* (1980) in Chapter 3). We have seen also that these reasons must be supported and not merely asserted – but that the level of proof required is not very high: *Banerjee* v. *City A.H.A.* (1979). Employers will welcome such latitude, but tribunals are presumably vigilant to see it is not abused. Another important aspect, to which we return in [7.10-7.11], is that when a business is transferred, dismissal on economic, technical or organisational grounds may go without redress because these are all regarded as substantial reasons for dismissal.

Other cases again may be cited which show more clearly the value and perhaps the proper purpose of the rule in enabling the employer to resolve conflicts of interest and other difficulties which could not otherwise be ended. In *Foot* v. *Eastern Counties Timber* (1972) the husband of a small firm's wages and accounts clerk started a rival business nearby. The firm had no complaint about their clerk's conduct or capacity, but inevitably she was now in a position where her domestic interests might conflict with her duties to her employer. The tribunal upheld her dismissal, but suggested in passing that she should have been given a testimonial confirming that she was in no way at fault. We might observe also that in cases like this, where the wife is dismissed on the basis that her husband is the breadwinner and dominant force in the household, there is a risk of liability for sex discrimination.

In *R.S. Components* v. *Irwin* (1973) a salesman's refusal to sign a new contract containing a reasonable restraint of trade term was held to be a substantial reason for dismissal, as was a manager's refusal in *Farr* v. *Hoveringham* (1972) to live closer to his work and be available in emergencies. *Parsons* v. *Norwich H.A.* (1982) concerned a student nurse who on conscientious grounds refused to take part in electroconvulsive therapy treatment. His good faith was said to rule out dismissal for misconduct, but the employer succeeded under the present heading because the treatment was laid down as an essential element of the course.

5.18 Third party pressures

A final specific area of interest is that of dismissals brought about by pressure from third parties such as customers or fellow employees. Tribunals accept that if customers say an employee is rude or fellow-employees find him highly objectionable in some way (other than because of his refusal to join a closed shop – a separate issue dealt with in [3.14] and [9.05]) – the employer may have little choice but to dismiss him. Ideally, he should investigate, give the employee the opportunity to explain, and consider what alternatives may be open: *Dobie* v. *Burns* (1984). In practice, and particularly if the employee knows his work is dependent upon a third party's approval, more drastic action may be unavoidable. An example is *Miller* v. *Strasburger* (1980) where dismissal was upheld because the employer had a concession counter at Selfridges, and

Selfridges insisted on the employee's dismissal.

Coombs v. *Tunbridge Wells Health Authority* (1984) is a last intriguing variation on the theme. Miss Coombs was a senior nursing officer who agreed with her employer to take early retirement but to be re-employed in important administrative work on a temporary and part-time basis. Following public disquiet about employees who took retirement benefits but continued working, the Secretary of State for Health, then Norman Fowler MP, sent a letter to all Health Authorities telling them to end any such contracts. The letter was not a legal direction or regulation. The Tunbridge Wells Authority objected on Miss Coombs' behalf, but was overruled and reluctantly dismissed her. Their defence to Miss Coombs' claim was that ministerial pressure was irresistible and therefore a substantial reason for dismissal. They said that although apparently autonomous employers, in reality they had to obey the Secretary's orders or else be punished by money being withheld, chairmen dismissed or 'other dire consequences'. The tribunal held that the Authority should have challenged the letter more strongly since it was not in legal form and required them to break their contracts for improper reasons – to maintain the Government's political popularity – and so held them liable. The tribunal ordered reinstatement, but the Secretary of State, nothing if not consistent in his disregard of the legal process, refused to allow it – which eventually cost taxpayers some £8000 in compensation for Miss Coombs.

Chapter 6

Procedural Fairness

6.01 The duty to act reasonably

We have now examined the four statutory good reasons – incapacity, misconduct, illegality and 'other substantial reason' – which justify dismissal without compensation, and we consider the separate and distinct issue of rights to redundancy payments in Chapter 7. But management is not only required to show a good reason for dismissal; it must also act fairly in the circumstances. This may sound like saying the same thing twice, but in fact emphasises the distinction between *why* one dismisses and *how* one goes about it. This requirement of procedural fairness affects all dismissals but certain aspects are more directly relevant to the grounds discussed in previous chapters. Tribunals are particularly concerned to know, for example, whether a warning should have been given before dismissal, or whether the employee had a fair hearing. The rule is explained as follows in section 57(3) of the Employment Protection (Consolidation) Act:

> 'Where the employer has [shown a good reason] ... the determination of the question whether the dismissal was fair or unfair, having regard to the reason shown by the employer, shall depend on whether in the circumstances (including the size and administrative resources of the employer's undertaking) the employer acted reasonably or unreasonably in treating it as a sufficient reason for dismissing the employee; and that question shall be determined in accordance with equity and the substantial merits of the case.'

Two interlocking questions thus arise: the meaning of 'reasonable' or 'unreasonable' action, and the effect upon the original ground for dismissal of any failure to act reasonably. We answer these questions by considering in turn the issues involved in investigation, hearing, rules, decision-making and appeal.

6.02 Investigation

An employer is not required to be absolutely certain of his facts before he dismisses: *A.E.I.* v. *McLay* (1980). If he alleges theft, for example, he will not be asked to prove his case 'beyond all reasonable doubt' at the tribunal as if he were prosecuting in the magistrates' court. He need show only a genuine belief, based on reasonable grounds: *Greenall Whitley* v. *Carr* (1985): see [6.04] below. Indeed, if he can show a genuine belief that one or two or more employees must be at fault, but cannot say which, he may be entitled to dismiss all. In *Monie* v. *Coral* (1980), only two people in the office could have taken the money but each denied liability and dismissal of both was upheld.

But genuine belief requires more than mere suspicion or rumour. The employer must make such inquiries as are reasonable in the circumstances, and will be deemed to know that which he ought to have known on proper investigation: *British Home Stores* v. *Burchell* (1978); *Weddel* v. *Tepper* (1980). In *Weddel* the Court of Appeal stated categorically that if employers form their opinions hastily and act hastily upon them, without making appropriate inquiries or giving employees a fair opportunity to explain themselves, their opinions are not based on reasonable grounds and they are not acting reasonably. Any resulting dismissal must therefore be unfair, unless of course it is abundantly clear that however hasty the decision it is nonetheless correct.

Burchell and *Weddel* do not, in other words, lay down inflexible rules to be applied in all cases. *Scottish Special Housing* v. *Linnen* (1979) held that where an employee has been caught red-handed, dismissal without further investigation may be appropriate. Similarly, in *Royal Society for the Protection of Birds* v. *Croucher* (1984) it was held that when an employee admits misconduct there is little scope or need for investigation to clear up doubt. But the fact that an employee has been charged with an offence by the police does not of itself preclude further investigation by the employer (or subsequent dismissal): *S.S.H.A.* v. *Cooke* (1979); *Harris* v. *Courage* (1982).

When detailed inquiries are necessary they will usually involve taking statements from all relevant witnesses and, in particular, from the employee under suspicion. Witnesses need not always be interviewed in the suspect's presence, though it is preferable that at some stage he has the opportunity to question them. Suspects should always be told in good time of the nature of the allegations against them and of their right to bring a friend or representative to the interview. Generally, they should not be interviewed when unable to give a proper account of themselves or under pressure – for example, due to the presence of police at the interview: *Read* v. *Phoenix* (1985). The strict technicalities of the rules of evidence do not apply, nor is there any precise form of procedure. In *Bentley* v. *Mistry* (1978) an employee was held unfairly dismissed for fighting, on the grounds that he had not been given written statements of witnesses nor the opportunity to cross-examine them. The Employment Appeal Tribunal said that while natural justice required that a man should know what was alleged against him and have the chance to state his own case in detail, this might, according to the facts, be achieved by written evidence, or by hearing what the other party says, or by an oral report of what others have said. 'There is no particular form of procedure that has to be followed in any and every case. It is all a question of degree.'

Cases illustrating unfairness in investigation include *Yate* v. *Walters* (1984), where a worker accused of playing cards was dismissed without any inquiry being made of another worker who, it was said, would confirm his version of events. In *Henderson* v. *Granville* (1982) a coach driver was summarily dismissed immediately after rejecting a long letter of complaint by a coach trip organiser as a 'load of rubbish'. The Employment Appeal Tribunal held that any reasonable employer would have given the driver more time to consider the letter, answer complaints and obtain statements, and would himself have made more inquiries. The fact that the company was a small one did not excuse failure to investigate customers' complaints properly. Dismissals were found unfair in both cases.

Inquiries and interviews should preferably be conducted at middle management level – for example, by a personnel officer – so as to leave open the possibility of appeal to a higher level of management not previously involved. It is obviously undesirable that the same person should undertake both investigation and final adjudication – a failing which contributed to liability in *Johnston* v. *East Surrey H.A.* (1983) – but certainly in smaller enterprises it may be difficult or impossible to secure a complete division of function. This problem was discussed at length in *Rowe* v. *Radio Rentals* (1982), below.

6.03   The hearing

It may be that at the end of the inquiry management feels sufficiently certain of itself simply to call in the employee and tell him he is fired. There is nothing inherently wrong with that so long as he has previously had the opportunity to defend himself, but it remains a somewhat speculative course of action. It is undoubtedly safer and more in accordance with what lawyers call the rules of natural justice to have a proper hearing in which witnesses give their evidence in the presence of the employee and his representative, and can be questioned on it by both sides. We observe in passing, however, that natural justice does not require all witnesses to be available for cross-examination. Written statements are quite acceptable if there is some good reason why the witnesses cannot be or do not wish to be present, as in *Khanum* v. *Mid Glamorgan A.H.A.* (1978) where hospital patients' written complaints against a nurse were upheld. It would have been extremely difficult to make them give their evidence in person, and in any case witnesses compelled to attend are unlikely to be very helpful. The E.A.T. said that in a domestic disciplinary inquiry such as this, natural justice required only that the employee should know the nature of the accusation against him, that he be given the opportunity to state his case, and that the domestic body should act in good faith.

6.04 Disciplinary rules

The purpose of the hearing is to find the relevant facts and then to apply the disciplinary rules. We have seen that the facts elicited need not be proof positive but such as to give the employer reasonable grounds for dismissal. We may recall also that in unfair (as distinct from wrongful) dismissal the employer's case stands or falls by what he knows at the time of dismissal. If the case is weak, he cannot support it by reference to information which comes to light only after employment is ended, other than through the domestic appeal procedure: *National Heart and Chest Hospitals* v. *Nambiar* (1981). The unfortunate result of this otherwise perfectly reasonable rule is illustrated in *Greenall Whitley* v. *Carr* (1985). An employee's explanation for discrepancies in a meter was rejected and he was dismissed for 'fiddling'. Subsequently it was found that his explanation might have been correct – but he was still held fairly dismissed on the evidence available at the time of dismissal. But if information acquired afterwards would have made dismissal inevitable, compensation is reduced accordingly: *Devis* v. *Atkins* (1977).

So far as the disciplinary rules themselves are concerned it is very much in the employer's interest to give time and thought to their preparation and application. Guidance is given by the ACAS Code of Practice on disciplinary practice and procedures in employment (Appendix 2) and the principles enlarged upon in the draft revision (Appendix 3). The Code emphasises that rules should be corrective as well as punitive. It recognises that employers cannot specify beforehand each and every form of misbehaviour or the penalty attached to it. 'The aim should be to specify clearly and concisely those [rules] necessary for the efficient and safe performance of work and for the maintenance of satisfactory relations.' Beyond that, employers should give 'a clear indication of the type of conduct which may warrant summary dismissal' – usually by listing four or five instances followed by a warning of dismissal for 'other forms of gross misconduct or incapacity', or words to that effect. The procedures laid down should be speedy but comprehensive, giving rights of information, representation and, if practicable, appeal. Power to dismiss should be confined to middle or senior management and not exercised on a first complaint except for gross misconduct. Generally, no serious action should be taken against a shop steward without reference to a more senior union official. The rules should be given to new employees and explained to them as part of the induction process – a useful way of emphasising their importance.

The very real difficulties in drafting workable rules were illustrated in *Meridian* v. *Gomersall* (1977). A company notice stated that employees guilty of clocking offences were 'liable to dismissal'. The E.A.T. held that dismissal was unfair because 'liable to' suggested that some lighter penalty might be imposed. But if the employer says instead that dismissal is inevitable he deprives himself of the discretion he needs to distinguish between major and minor transgressions of the rule or to take account of extenuating circumstances. Later cases such as *Elliot* v. *Colverd* (1979) take the more realistic view that an employer's liability should not depend on fine shades of meaning which might be attributed to workaday rules whose basic purpose and effect is reasonably clear.

6.05   The decision

If his complaint against his employee is substantiated, the employer must consider the range of possible penalties. Whether dismissal is appropriate depends as we have said on whether it is within the band of reasonable responses of a reasonable employer – a standard which gives management a very wide discretion. The decision to dismiss may be reached in part by reference to previous incidents and warnings involving that employee. If so, it is desirable that the past incidents are of broadly the same nature as that now in question, and that they occurred in the not too distant past. The ACAS Code suggests that, except in agreed special circumstances, breaches of disciplinary rules should be disregarded after a specified period of satisfactory conduct. But there is no rule of law to that effect, and ultimately the question is simply one of the relevance or otherwise of the employee's record. There is no reason why past misbehaviour of a completely different kind should not contribute to a present general impression of unreliability.

Similarly, when previous warnings are invoked to justify dismissal, it is helpful but not essential that they relate to recent and comparable behaviour. For ease of proof, warnings should always be in writing, but are not invalid merely because they are spoken: *McCall* v. *Castleton* (1979). Warnings should ideally be more than vague injunctions to 'pull your socks up'. They should tell the employee what is expected of him and give him time to put things right. But, equally, employees must be prepared to take a hint. In *Judge* v. *Moss* (1973), for instance, a group secretary asked why he had not had a salary increase. He was told: 'Your performance does not justify one' – and that was held to be an effective warning.

Once a 'final warning' has been given, the employer is usually justified in dismissing on any recurrence or further unsatisfactory conduct. But two reservations might be borne in mind. First, it is always possible that the final warning was itself inappropriate; perhaps an over-reaction to a forgivable error, as in *Herdman Grant*: see [4.05]. If so, the warning could not be relied upon. But the mere fact that a warning is under appeal does not preclude dismissal. Second, even the most well-deserved of warnings should not be used to justify dismissal for a subsequent incident which in itself is of no consequence and would not normally attract disciplinary proceedings.

When deciding whether to warn or dismiss, the employer will have in mind also that the ACAS Code advises against dismissal for a first offence other than gross misconduct and suggests oral and then written warnings in lieu. It must be emphasised, however, that while warnings may be the norm they are not by any means every employee's legal entitlement. Misconduct or incapacity, illegality or other substantial reason for dismissal, of the gravity illustrated in some of the cases in the two preceding chapters, justifies dismissal even for a first offence. If the employer is confident of the justice and necessity of dismissal he is unlikely to be found liable for failure to warn instead, unless perhaps he can be accused of inconsistency.

Consistency of treatment is an important element of fairness, not only for its own sake but because it tells employees the likely consequences of their acts. Charges of inconsistency are often made, but rarely stick. They are irrelevant unless the circumstances of each case are virtually identical, or 'truly parallel' as was said in *Hadjioannou* v. *Coral* (1981). One employee might be suspended for theft and another dismissed, but that alone would not prove unequal treatment. The value of the goods might be entirely different or the responsibility of the second employee so much greater, or the employer might have warned everybody after the first incident that the next offender would be dismissed. The answer an employer ought to be able to give to a charge of inconsistency is that all employees are treated equally, in the sense that each case is dealt with on its own merits.

6.06   Appeal

A vital component of a domestic disciplinary procedure, if at all practicable, is a right of appeal, and correspondingly that the employee should be told of that right. A second and preferably independent view is valuable in itself, and also provides a way of remedying minor defects in the original hearing. But in a small firm only 'the boss' can dismiss in the first place, and so the absence of an appeal could not make dismissal unfair. The presence or absence of such procedures thus becomes just one of many factors to be considered: *Shannon* v. *Michelin* (1981). If the employee chooses not to exercise his right that does not prove his dismissal fair.

Even in larger enterprises there is always the possibility that the same people will be involved in both dismissal and appeal proceedings, with the consequent appearance of prejudice. A leading case on this problem is *Rowe* v. *Radio Rentals* (1982). After dismissal by the area manager, the employee appealed to the regional manager. The area manager put the case against him to the regional manager, and stayed throughout the hearing. The employee complained that bias was inevitable in these circumstances.

The Employment Appeal Tribunal said it was very important that internal appeals procedures run by commercial enterprises should not be cramped by impracticable legal requirements. It was almost inevitable that the person who made the original decision to dismiss would be in daily contact with his superiors who would hear the appeal, and would probably have to put the facts of the case to him. The tribunal concluded that: 'Rules about total separation of functions and lack of contact between those hearing the appeal and those involved in the original decision therefore cannot be applied in the majority of cases'. As long as the disciplinary and appeal bodies acted fairly and justly their decisions were to be supported. The employee therefore lost his case.

6.07 The effect of procedural faults

These, then, are the elements of fair dismissal procedures, together with their recognised limitations. We can now begin to answer our second question – as to the consequences of failure to follow such procedures.

We should understand first that neither the ACAS Code nor the employer's own procedure, whether or not agreed with the union, is legally enforceable. Procedures are expressions of what is fair and desirable, but compliance is essentially optional. Failure to follow them cannot of itself make dismissal unfair. In any case, the validity or otherwise of the actual reason for dismissal must normally be far more important than the way dismissal was carried out. But the possibility still remains that it may have been handled so badly as to vitiate the whole proceedings. The industrial tribunal's task is then to distinguish between procedural faults which matter and those which do not, which in turn is one more aspect of the overall standard of fairness they are there to enforce.

Their approach is illustrated in the following cases, starting with a minor but clear-cut example. In *Brady* v. *Leeds A.H.A.* (1976) a nurse was sacked when found drunk in charge of a ward. She said this was unfair partly because her copy of the disciplinary code did not give the name or rank of person entitled to dismiss her, as the Code says it should. The tribunal thought this particular procedural shortfall was so trivial that it could not possibly affect Mrs Brady's basic breach of duty and so upheld her dismissal – a decision with which it would be hard to disagree.

A more important case is *Stewart* v. *Western S.M.T.* (1978). Under the agreed procedure, employees who misconducted themselves were to be counselled immediately by their supervisors. Mr Stewart left work early without clocking off, contrary to orders.

Instead of being counselled, he was watched and seen to commit the same offence twice more. He was then dismissed without warning. The Tribunal held that the counselling requirement really applied only to minor offences and could not prevent dismissal for serious ones. Since he could properly have been dismissed for the first offence the employers were free to disregard their agreement.

In *Wass* v. *Binns* (1982), a border-line case with a strong dissenting judgment in the Court of Appeal, it was held unnecessary to interview a lorry driver to get his side of the story, which would have included medical anxieties not previously mentioned, after his offensive and unexplained refusal to take his lorry out. But the Court agreed that an interview was usually an appropriate precaution. Similarly in *Silliphant* v. *Powell Duffryn* (1983) an employee accused of theft was dismissed without the opportunity to defend himself, but since the evidence against him was overwhelming nothing he could have said would have made any difference and so dismissal was fair.

Other leading cases to the same effect include *British Labour Pump* v. *Byrne* (1979), which concerned a shop steward dismissed for theft after a virtual admission of guilt. Dismissal was nonetheless held unfair because there was no detailed investigation of the circumstances, no union representative involved as the Code says there should be, and the disciplinary committee was not convened. But he lost half his compensation because there was evidently a good case against him. In *Post Office* v. *Strange* (1980) an employee was not allowed to appeal against a penalty to the regional director as provided in the disciplinary procedure. He was thereby deprived of an independent rehearing of his case, and resigned in protest. It was held that this was too important a right to be overlooked and that he was unfairly constructively dismissed. Similarly, in *West Midlands Co-operative Society* v. *Tipton* (1986), the House of Lords held that an employer's refusal in breach of contract to allow an employee his right of appeal made the dismissal unfair even though it had originally been justified. *Gibson* v. *British Transport* (1982) shows that management's failure to consider individual cases fully when dismissing several employees for alleged violent picketing must necessarily be unfair, though the employees lost 90 per cent of their compensation because of the evidence of violence and subsequent lying about it.

6.08 Conclusion

In effect, then, the tribunal must ask itself whether the employer's failure to follow procedure would have made any difference to the outcome: *Siggs* v. *Knight* (1984). To put that another way, if it is clear the outcome would have been the same if the procedure had been followed, failure to follow it cannot matter. That is not by any means to say that procedure is unimportant, nor that employers need not make every effort to follow the rules. Many cases are marginal, and there is no point in risking liability by appearing to behave arbitrarily.

Chapter 7

Redundancy

7.01 Introduction

Our main concern so far has been to advise employers how to avoid liability for unfair dismissal. But if the cause of dismissal is redundancy, liability is inescapable – subject to the conditions of entitlement laid down in the Employment Protection (Consolidation) Act 1978 and set out below.

7.02 Unfair redundancy

First, however, we note the possibility of 'unfair redundancy'. This occurs where there is no dispute that *someone* must be made redundant, but the employer cannot prove that the person selected was chosen fairly. Fairness here involves observance of a 'customary arrangement or agreed procedure', e.g. 'last in, first out', as laid down by section 59 of the 1978 Act. Tacit or implied selection agreements with unions are included: *Henry* v. *Ellerman Lines* (1985). A departure from the agreement can only be justified if as section 59 says there is some 'special reason,' but that excludes mere financial difficulties facing the employer: *Cross* v. *Reid* (1985). This basic procedural rule is intended to stop employers who want to get rid of employees on perhaps more personal grounds from using redundancy as a pretext. An employer who cannot justify his method of selection for redundancy will be faced with a claim for compensation for unfair dismissal which will almost certainly cost him much more than a redundancy claim.

It follows that employers should be able to point to some objective criteria for selection and to due regard for industrial relations. These requirements are stressed by Employment Appeal Tribunal decisions such as *Freud* v. *Bentalls* and *Williams* v. *Compair Maxam*, both of 1982, which underline particularly the wisdom of giving as much notice as possible to both employee and union, consulting jointly and seeking alternative employment for those displaced. Part Five of the draft ACAS Code of Practice on disciplinary and other procedures in employment (Appendix 3) enlarges on these principles, first stated in the Industrial Relations Code of Practice issued under the ill-fated Industrial Relations Act 1971. But the principles are not hard and fast rules to be applied in all cases, as the draft makes clear. Their application depends on what is desirable or practicable in a given situation: *Grundy* v. *Plummer* (1983). Apparently objective methods of selection may be unreasonable in themselves, such as those based on age: *Farthing* v. *Midland Stores* (1974). Or an employer may find a 'last in, first out' policy unworkable because he wants to keep skilled men, and not have to get rid of them simply because he has only just recruited them. Elements of subjective assessment are probably unavoidable, but still acceptable if they are explained in advance and involve demonstrable personal merit on the one hand or avoidance of hardship on the other rather than mere personal preference.

Detailed proof of the accuracy of information relied on by management for these purposes is not usually required. The tribunals will not interfere if they are persuaded that an employer's assessment in any given case is 'within the band of reasonable responses' to the situation, though they may seek *prima facie* evidence that redundancy is necessary in the first place.

Williams, above, illustrates very well how selection for redundancy may be unfair. After many years' service the employee was made redundant without any prior notice and in accordance merely with the manager's personal view of the best interests of the company. He was therefore awarded compensation for unfair dismissal rather than redundancy pay. If redundancy makes dismissal inevitable, however, and it is only the method of selection or failure to consult which makes it unfair, compensation may be reduced or refused: *Crowson* v. *Kraft* (1983). Selection of part-timers rather than full-timers may be unfair even though in accordance with a union agreement, because it might be an indirect form of sex discrimination: *Clarke* v. *Eley*, (1982). This view, however, was disputed in *Kidd* v. *K.R.G.* (1985) where it was said this was a proposition which had to be proved rather than merely assumed valid. Selection because of union membership or non-membership is automatically unfair (section 59 of the 1978 Act).

Dismissal will also be unfair unless the employer can show he has considered whatever alternatives may be available. The original Code of Practice of 1972 urged that less overtime and more short-time working should be considered – a suggestion repeated in the draft ACAS Code (Appendix 3). Failure to take these possibilities into account led to liability for unfair dismissal in *Lloyd* v. *Standard Fuel* (1976). The employer must also look for possible openings in his own company or associated companies: *Vokes* v. *Bear* (1973). It is for the employee rather than the employer to decide upon their suitability. But if other jobs are not available the employer has no duty to create them.

In contrast we might note three controversial cases where dismissal for redundancy was held to be fair. In *Cruickshank* v. *Hobbs* (1977) certain employees were chosen for redundancy because they had just been on strike. The employer's decision was upheld because redundancy was unavoidable and not used as a pretext, and he had a responsibility to support those who had stayed at work. Selection for redundancy because of a bad work record and without warning was held fair in *Gray* v. *Shetland Norse* (1985) because the primary reason was redundancy and it said that 'Williams' guidelines only applied to large-scale redundancies involving negotiations with unions. It may also be fair to dismiss under an agreement providing for 'bumping' or 'transferred redundancy'. This enables the employer to transfer a redundant employee to another job and dismiss the employee who is thereby displaced: *Elliott* v. *Bates* (1981).

CONDITIONS OF ENTITLEMENT

7.03   (1) Employment within the Act

The basic qualification for redundancy pay is two years' service between the ages of eighteen and sixty-five (or sixty for women) under a contract requiring more than sixteen hours' work a week, or five years' under a contract for more than eight hours' work a week. These are the same requirements as for protection against unfair dismissal, and so we need not add immediately to what we said about them in Chapter 3. We shall enlarge upon the rules later when considering how redundancy pay is calculated and the circumstances in which employment with different employers may be deemed continuous: see [7.10–7.12] below.

Employees outside the scope of the Act are Crown employees, holders of certain public offices, NHS employees, registered dock workers, share fishermen, employees – other than British seamen – who normally work outside Britain unless in Britain at the time of dismissal on their employer's instructions, and domestic servants closely related to their employers – excluding uncles, aunts, nephews and nieces. A person employed under a fixed term contract of two years or more loses his right to redundancy pay if he agrees in writing beforehand not to make a claim when the term expires. Several occupations, including NHS workers, dockers and miners have their own statutory schemes. All disputes are decided by industrial tribunals.

7.04   (2) Dismissal

No claim can be made unless there has been a dismissal. This is defined in the same way as for unfair dismissal – termination with or without notice by the employer, constructive dismissal, and non-renewal of a fixed term contract – all of which we discussed in detail in [3.07–3.11]. There is no dismissal where the employee is warned that redundancy is imminent and so leaves to get another job. Strictly speaking he leaves of his own accord in that situation, and so has no claim: *Doble* v. *Firestone Co.* (1981). The Industrial Relations Code of Practice and draft ACAS Code urge the employer to give as much advance warning of redundancy as possible, but as and when the employee heeds the warning and finds work elsewhere he should be advised to ask formally to be dismissed. An employee under notice may give a written counter-notice of intention to leave after one week. If the employer accepts the counter-notice the employee is still regarded as dismissed for redundancy, but if he leaves against his employer's wishes he may lose part or all of his entitlement.

A helpful example of constructive dismissal in the redundancy context is *Marriott* v. *Oxford Co-operative Soc.* (1969). A supervisor of six men was told that because work was declining he would thenceforth have charge only of three, would have to do some manual work and suffer a cut in pay. These unilateral changes amounted to termination of his contract by the employer, entitling him to leave and claim redundancy pay. The decision is clear enough in itself, but it is sometimes very difficult to distinguish between cases of this kind where the tribunal finds a fundamental breach or repudiation of the contract by the employer, justifying the employee's claim for compensation, and those which are said to involve only organisational changes brought about by 'sound, good business reasons'. Such necessary 'adjustments' may well involve breaches of contract, but they are of a less fundamental nature. Employees must therefore accept them, or, if they leave, go without redress. These 'quasi-redundancy' cases were discussed in [5.05] and the problem is pursued below in [7.07]. Reference should also be made to resignations following short-time working or lay-off (see [7.08]).

7.05   (3) Redundancy

The crucial question, then, is the cause of dismissal. Section 81 of the 1978 Act says that it is for redundancy if wholly or mainly attributable to:

'(a) the fact that his employer has ceased, or intends to cease, to carry on the business for the purposes of which the employee was employed by him, or has ceased, or intends to cease, to carry on that business in the place where the employee was so employed, or (b) the fact that the requirements of that business for employees to carry out work of a particular kind, or for employees to carry out work of a particular kind in the place where he was so employed, have ceased or diminished or are expected to cease or diminish.'

The word 'business' is defined in section 153 of the Act to include a trade or profession and 'any activity carried on by a body of persons, whether corporate or unincorporate'.

Dismissal in any of the circumstances above is deemed due to redundancy. If liability to make a redundancy payment is to be avoided the employer must show some other cause such as incapacity or misconduct. It is for the tribunal to decide the real reason for dismissal, and so the employee can claim alternatively compensation for unfair dismissal or redundancy pay.

7.06 Purposes and place of employment

The definition above asks first whether those purposes of the business for which the employee was engaged have come or are about to come to an end, temporarily or permanently, at his place of employment. As regards the purposes of employment there is always the possibility that an employee's contract may seem to make him employable for more than one purpose, perhaps by means of what we called in Chapter 1 an *et cetera* clause. We have seen that these clauses are quite narrowly interpreted and unlikely to compel employees to move to entirely different jobs. So in *Cowen* v. *Haden* (1982) a contract requiring the employee to fulfil 'any duties reasonably within his capabilities' obliged him only to undertake work essentially similar to his original employment. If sufficiently specific in its demands, however, the transferability clause may certainly be effective, as in *Bex* v. *Securicor* (1972): see [5.05].

A similar question may arise with regard to the place of work. If an employee's contract enables his employer to move him from one place of work to another, he is not redundant merely because one

such place closes: *U.K. Atomic Energy Authority* v. *Claydon* (1974).
If he refuses to go when contractually obliged to do so he can be
dismissed for misconduct. It is therefore very much in employers'
interests to write whatever mobility demands they may wish to
make expressly and clearly into their contracts. Such clauses may
sometimes be implied by law, but employers should not need to
rely upon that possibility: see [5.05].

7.07   Requirements for work of a particular kind

The definition of redundancy requires the tribunal to decide in any
given case whether the employer has made what might be called a
new demand for a new job. If so, the person displaced is redundant.
But if what the employer wants is essentially a new version of the
old job – a reorganisation or updating of the process – there is, as we
said earlier, no redundancy and any employee who cannot or will
not adapt stands to lose his job. He will be dismissed for the
'substantial reason' that he has refused to accept necessary
variations in conditions of employment. The law evidently gives
employees much less protection here than it seems to. An example
is *Chapman* v. *Goonvean* (1973) where the Court of Appeal held
that withdrawal of a free transport concession did not effectively
alter the original job. Lord Denning said:

> 'It is very desirable in the interests of efficiency that employers
> should be able to propose changes in the terms of a man's
> employment for such reasons as these: so as to get rid of
> restrictive practices; or to induce higher output by piece work; or
> to cease to provide free transport at an excessive cost'.

How then do we distinguish work of one 'particular kind' from
another? The answer given in *Amos* v. *Max-Arc* (1973) is that work
of a particular kind is 'distinguished from other work of the same
general kind by requiring special aptitudes, skill or knowledge'. It
follows that if one job stops and men are transferred to another they
are not thereby entitled to redundancy pay because the skills may
be the same. And, conversely, the fact that an employee has the skill
to do another job does not prove he was taken on to do it.

The cases turn very much on their own facts. We can do little more than give examples where the tribunals have found 'new jobs', thus giving rise to redundancy claims, and those where they have found only reorganisational requirements. In *Murphy* v. *Epsom College* (1984) the college heating system had been looked after by the college plumber. A new and more complex system was installed which needed the full-time services of a 'heating technician', who could also deal with plumbing problems. This was held to be a new and more highly skilled job, which made the plumber redundant. Changing job requirements from day shift to night or vice versa is regarded as creating a new job: *Macfisheries* v. *Findlay* (1985) whereas reducing hours as a result of 'adjustments in production' – *Yusuf* v. *Aberplace* (1985) – or changing a five-day week to a six-day shift system, as in *Johnson* v. *Nottinghamshire Police Authority* (1974), does not fundamentally affect existing work. Converting a part-time job into a full-time one likewise does not give rise to redundancy if there is no change in the demand for the work itself: *Banerjee* v. *City A.H.A.* (1979). It is for employers to set the standards they require, but tribunals must take account of the reasonableness or otherwise of employees' refusal to accept them: *Spencer* v. *Gloucestershire C.C.* (1985).

The Employment Appeal Tribunal held in *O'Hare* v. *Rotaprint* (1980) that where an employer takes on more workers in the belief that work is expanding he should not be penalised by having to make redundancy payments if things turn out badly. Temporary over-manning may not mean that the requirements of the business have changed. Against this, the Court of Appeal decided in *Nottinghamshire C.C.* v. *Lee* (1980), in the same year, that when employment originally agreed upon as temporary because of declining demand duly comes to an end, redundancy is established. It seems difficult to reconcile these cases, and *O'Hare* may have to be reconsidered.

If reorganisation is intended to reduce the number of employees, or replace them with independent contractors, those dismissed are redundant: *Robinson* v. *British Island Airways* (1977). The same is true of replacement of men by women or vice versa. On the other hand, the dismissal of an elderly barmaid in *Vaux* v. *Ward* (1969) because her employer now had a policy of employing 'bunny girls' did not entitle her to redundancy pay because basically the work remained the same – though one might still have thought that different 'aptitudes' were contemplated.

Another type of problem arises where skill requirements gradually change, though without any specific demand by the employer, or where older workers find it more and more difficult to adapt. In *Hindle* v. *Percival Boats* (1969) an elderly craftsman lost his job because he was 'too good and too slow'. He was not redundant, since there had been no specific change in the requirements of the business, but was in effect incompetent in the sense that he could not keep up with production rates. Both *Hindle's* case and *Vaux* v. *Ward*, above, were decided before the concept of unfair dismissal was introduced. Dismissal in such circumstances nowadays might possibly be regarded as unfair, but there is certainly no duty upon an employer to find new jobs for everyone displaced by reorganisation. We might observe also from *Hindle* that if, as there, the reason for an employee's dismissal is not redundancy it does not then become redundancy if and insofar as the employer finds he need not replace him. And, conversely, an employee might still be redundant even though replaced immediately by others with different skills.

7.08   (4) Short-time or lay-off

We have seen that employees must wait to be dismissed before they can claim redundancy pay. That could cause considerable hardship in the event of lay-offs or short-time working. The employee might resign and claim constructive dismissal in these circumstances, but his claim would necessarily be speculative. Sections 87-89 of the 1978 Act therefore enable employees who for any reason other than an industrial dispute are laid off or put on short-time (earning less than half their normal weekly pay) for four consecutive weeks or any six weeks in thirteen to give in their notice but still qualify as dismissed. To come within the rules they must give written 'notice of intent to claim' within one month of the last relevant week of short-time or lay-off. If the employer has reasonable grounds for believing normal work will resume within four weeks and continue for at least three months he may give a written counter-notice which warns the employee that if he goes ahead and gives in his notice his claim for redundancy pay will be contested. Contracts of employment in building and other seasonal industries may expressly entitle employers to lay off without pay. Such provision does not affect employees' rights to claim under these sections: *McRae* v. *Dawson* (1984).

7.09 (5) Renewal of contract or suitable alternative employment

After giving notice, but before employment comes to an end, an employer may offer to renew a worker's contract on the same terms as before or to provide suitable alternative employment. By law the offer may be oral or in writing, but in practice all such transactions should be recorded in writing. It must take effect not more than four weeks after employment ends (extended to the fourth Monday if employment ends on a Friday, Saturday or Sunday) and, if accepted, continuity of employment is preserved. If the employee unreasonably refuses the offer he loses his right to redundancy pay: section 82. The same rules apply to offers by new or associated employers, as explained below: see also [7.11].

On the face of it an offer of re-employment on the same terms presents little difficulty, so long as the offer is clear. If it is refused the onus is on the employer to prove refusal unreasonable – *Jones* v. *Aston* (1973), a difficult point to which we return below. Arguments are more likely to arise over offers of alternative employment – which means employment in which *the capacity and place in which the employee works and other terms of his contract differ wholly or partly from those previously agreed* (section 82).

The first question will then be to decide whether the proposed changes did, in fact, represent a new job, or were merely changes in accordance with the terms of the original contract. We have mentioned already the duty of compliance imposed by express or implied mobility clauses: see [5.05] and [7.06]. If a particular contract does not contain such a clause then the suitability of the new offer as regards capacity, place, etc., depends on the circumstances of the individual case, and again we can do no more than illustrate the possibilities.

Suitability has been held to be a matter of 'substantial equivalence', taking into account status, pay, overtime opportunities, travel and the like. Reductions in status are not usually acceptable, though much depends on the length of time the higher post has been held.

In *Taylor* v. *Kent C.C.* (1969) a headmaster was made redundant and offered alternative work as a supply teacher, but at his former rate of pay. It was held that preservation of pay could not compensate for such loss of status and so the offer was completely unsuitable. Reductions in pay and security may have to be accepted. An employee might be justified in refusing a temporary job, but could not demand a guarantee of permanence: *James* v. *N.C.B.* (1969). Changes in shift hours are not in themselves unsuitable but may become so if they create domestic or travelling or other such difficulties.

One must be realistic also in deciding whether the place of work has been changed to any significant extent. 'Where the employer merely moves into a building next door, can it be said that this is a termination of a contract of employment? We think not': *Stevens* v. *Stitcher* (1966). Requiring an employee to move from Holborn to Regent Street in London was held not to involve any fundamental breach of contract in *Managers* v. *Hohne* (1977), though on similar facts *Air Canada* v. *Lee* (1978) reached an opposite conclusion. The decision no doubt turns on whether the move creates travelling difficulties and expense or, for example, reduces overtime opportunities.

Rose v. *Trickett* (1971) suggests that employees should be given the benefit of the doubt on these questions of fact and degree. Here employees of a building firm continued in service with new owners of the firm, doing the same kind of work and subject as before to the industry's national working rules. But their new contracts were oral instead of written, and included minor variations in their pay, overtime, hours, expenses and holiday pay. The right approach, said the court, was not to look at the contracts as packages but at individual terms. Some changes might be so trivial as to be ignored, but the changes here amounted to new contracts.

Once an employee has accepted new terms he cannot then deny their suitability. But what constitutes acceptance? There must be no compulsion, nor can it be presumed that an employee asked by his employer to stay on and help to run the firm down before closure 'accepts' the resulting lower rate of pay: *Saxton* v. *N.C.B.* (1970). If, on the other hand, more work is demanded at a higher rate, that higher rate will in due course become the basis of the new contract: *Armstrong* v. *Mustard* (1971).

Section 84 of the 1978 Act encourages the employee to try out the new contract for a trial period of four weeks, or any longer period agreed beforehand in writing which states also the terms and conditions applying after that period. If the employee works the full trial period he cannot then say the job is unsuitable: *Meek* v. *Allen* (1980). If he refuses the offer in the first place, or leaves during the trial period, he does so at his own risk. But if the tribunal agrees that the new work is unsuitable or his refusal to try it reasonable, his right to redundancy pay is unaffected.

Alternatively, the employee may argue that if he is ordered to do a new job in breach of his former contract he is thereby justified in resigning and claiming compensation for unfair constructive dismissal. In these circumstances the tribunals will allow him a 'reasonable time' to consider his position and try out the new job without thereby losing his statutory right to a trial period: *Turvey* v. *Cheyney* (1979).

Finally under the present heading is the question of the reasonableness of the employee's refusal to undertake what might otherwise be suitable alternative employment. While the tribunals tend to judge job suitability objectively they accept that reasons for refusal may be very personal, though they must still be substantial. An employee might properly refuse identical work elsewhere for such reasons as ill-health or dependent relatives, or because he had just bought a house near his work, or his children's schooling would be seriously affected. It may also be reasonable to refuse an offer because he has already found another job. Personal preferences as to acceptable standards of service or agreeable environments are unlikely to be seen as good reasons for refusal: *Spencer* v. *Gloucestershire C.C.* (1985); *Fuller* v. *Bowman* (1977). In the latter case it was held that the employee had no right to refuse employment in an office over a sex shop.

7.10   (6) Continuity of service

Unfair dismissal and redundancy pay claims both depend on showing two years' continuity of service under contracts requiring more than sixteen hours' work a week, or five years under contracts for more than eight hours a week. In both contexts, therefore, important questions arise as to the effects of interruptions in service and in particular as to employees' rights when a new employer takes over. We deal with these issues here because they are more important in relation to redundancy, where long service brings larger payments, but their application to unfair dismissal should be borne in mind.

The following rules are laid down in Schedule 13 of the 1978 Act. Continuity of service is not affected by up to 26 weeks' absence for illness or injury, plus any contractual entitlement to sick leave. The same is true of absence because of pregnancy, and if the employee returns to work thereafter up to forty weeks' absence is allowed. Continuity under a 'sixteen hour' contract is preserved for up to twenty-six weeks if weekly hours fall to not less than eight. Dismissal followed immediately by re-engagement on the same terms or within four weeks by suitable alternative employment does not affect continuity. Employers also remain liable *even though the contract has been ended* if employees are dismissed because of illness but re-engaged within twenty-six weeks, or because of temporary stoppages of work, or if by arrangement or custom they are regarded as continuing in employment.

This latter provision is particularly important where work is temporary or seasonal. It is not necessary to prove an express agreement or clear custom as to re-engagement. The parties' intentions are decided by the tribunal in the light of what has actually happened between them: *Fitzgerald* v. *Hall Russell* (1970). Periods of weeks or even months, in which the employee may have taken a temporary job elsewhere, have been found within the rule. A notable case is *Ford* v. *Warwickshire C.C.* (1983), where a teacher was employed under a succession of fixed term contracts from September to July. The House of Lords held that the arrangement or custom between teacher and employer was such as to preserve continuity from one contract to the next. Each case turns entirely on its own facts, however, and the difficulties of prediction are well illustrated by two Employment Appeal Tribunal decisions given within days of each other on apparently very similar facts but with different conclusions. In *Hellyer* v. *McLeod* (1985), trawlermen who signed off at the end of each voyage with the same company were held to have been employed under successive short-term contracts and not one global contract beginning with their first voyage. Yet in *Boyd* v. *Pitts* (1985) a trawlerman who had worked exclusively for one employer for many years but signed off and drew unemployment pay after each voyage was held continuously employed throughout. This seems the more appropriate and likely view of such circumstances. If after dismissal a tribunal orders reinstatement, then again employment is continuous, but it may not necessarily be so if the order is only to re-engage: see [9.01–9.03].

Time spent on strike affects continuity only in the limited sense that it does not count towards overall length of service. The same applies to time spent abroad if no national insurance contributions are payable, and to time in military service. Any other interruptions end the contract, and so if and when the employee returns to that employment he must begin again to accumulate years of service.

7.11   Change of employer

Continuity is also called into question by changes in the ownership of a business. Paragraph 17 of Schedule 13 says that continuity is preserved:

(i) where a trade, business or undertaking is transferred;
(ii) where at the time of transfer the new employer was an 'associated employer' of the former employer;
(iii) where one 'body corporate' supersedes another under Act of Parliament (as, for example, under local authority or Health Service reorganisation);
(iv) where an employer dies and the business is continued by his personal representatives or trustees;
(v) where new partners are introduced into a partnership.

We discuss below what is meant by 'transfer of a business', but note first the short point concerning 'associated employers': item

(ii) above. Under section 153 of the Act, employers are associated if one is a company directly or indirectly controlled by the other, or if both are companies directly or indirectly controlled by a third person. The case of *Umar* v. *Pliastar* (1981) reaches the somewhat unrealistic but convenient conclusion that control is to be measured strictly by majority voting rights rather than by exercise of power or influence. The significance of the definition of association is that employees in nationalised industries, local government and other such organisations which seem to have community of interest and are ultimately responsible to one person, a government minister, cannot usually claim continuity of service because none of these bodies is a company. For redundancy payment purposes, however, exceptions are made for local government and Health Service employees. Outside the area of unfair dismissal rights all these bodies are, of course, free to agree by collective bargaining with their respective unions that service with one employer can be joined to service with another for the benefits of seniority, pension rights, etc., and this is commonly done.

The more complex question affects the rights and duties of the parties on transfer of a business, item (i) above. Continuity of service is preserved on transfer only if the new employer takes over the business as a going concern, and not if he merely buys its assets for use in some entirely different activity. If there is no transfer, continuity is broken when the assets change hands: *Melon* v. *Powe* (1980). Employees unaware that they should claim against their former employers in these circumstances lose their rights to claim after six months. And if they remain at work at the new employer's request, any claim for redundancy payment can be based only on the time spent with him.

It is difficult to say how similar the old and new businesses must be to preserve continuity, and not the sort of question most employees would think to ask. In *Woodhouse* v. *Brotherhood* (1972) a heavy engineering firm sold out to a medium engineering firm, which kept the former's employees. These were held to be fundamentally different businesses and not both just engineering companies. Since continuity was thus broken, the employee was entitled to redundancy pay from his new employer only for the short time spent with him. In *Crompton* v. *Truly Fair* (1975) the same distinction was drawn between manufacture of children's clothes and subsequent use of the premises and plant by a new employer to make men's trousers. The effect on this occasion was to uphold the employee's claim for redundancy pay against her first employer. Another example is *Bumstead* v. *John* (1977) where the employee worked at a petrol station for a series of employers, but each had obtained only the right to sell petrol there, not the business itself, and so there was no continuity. On the other hand, the Employment Appeal Tribunal held in *Jeetle* v. *Elster* (1985) that continuity was preserved when after the dissolution of a partnership a partnership employee remained in the service of one of the former partners.

Where continuity is broken, the new employer sometimes promises to preserve existing employees' rights to encourage them to stay on. If so, his promise could only be enforced in a county court breach of contract action, not by an industrial tribunal, and if it were so enforced the new employer could not claim redundancy rebate because he would not have acted in accordance with the statutory provisions.

7.12   Transfer of Undertakings Regulations

The conclusions above seem equally unsatisfactory for both sides. The Transfer of Undertakings (Protection of Employment) Regulations 1981 attempted to make the position clearer and more secure for employees, but superimposed as they are on the existing rules they do not by any means resolve the problems.

The Regulations apply to sales or other disposals of businesses (including transfers by receivers or liquidators to subsidiary companies) unless brought about by sale of shares. This is a major exception; the reason for it presumably being that acquiring a business by purchase of shares does not alter its legal identity. Regulation 5 provides that when a business changes hands in any other way those employed in it immediately before the transfer (a phrase which disregards breaks of only a day or two) automatically become employees of the new owner. Their contractual rights against the old employer are preserved against the new one, apart from occupational pension rights. Collective agreements and union recognition rights are likewise protected. But the new employer is not responsible for non-contractual obligations such as the former employer's duty to pay a protective award, below. Any attempt to contract out of the Regulations is void. The immediate effect is that employees cannot claim redundancy pay on transfers within the Regulations, and no longer need to, because such transfers have no effect on continuity. If there are substantial and detrimental changes in his existing terms of employment the employee can resign and claim constructive dismissal. The employer's change of identity is not normally such a substantial or detrimental change.

The most controversial aspect of these rules is in Regulation 8. This says first that employees dismissed because of the transfer, whether before or after it, shall be treated as unfairly dismissed. It then qualifies that by saying that if dismissal is for an 'economic, technical or organisational reason entailing changes in the workforce [it] shall be regarded as having been for a substantial reason of a kind such as to justify the dismissal of an employee holding [that] position'. This wording repeats that in section 57 of the 1978 Act making dismissal for a 'substantial reason' fair.

The effect of this provision is far from clear. 'Economic, technical or organisational' reasons would appear wide enough to justify virtually any dismissal by a new owner, and initially at least this was the veiw of the tribunals. In *Meikle* v. *McPhail* (1983), for example, the respondent employer took over a public house, contracting also to keep its existing employees. He found immediately that economies were necessary and dismissed all but one of the staff within four days. One of those dismissed was a barmaid. She was given a payment for redundancy but claimed compensation for unfair dismissal. The Employment Appeal Tribunal in Scotland rejected her claim because she was dismissed on 'economic' grounds which according to the Regulations were a 'substantial' and therefore valid reason for dismissal. The new employer's folly in buying the business in the first place did not help the applicant. 'Many employees have to be dismissed as a result of incompetent business management', said the tribunal, 'but this does not make the dismissal unfair'. The court held that there was no right to redundancy pay either because redundancy was another 'substantial reason' within the Regulations. But since the circumstances were akin to redundancy, employers' duties in that respect also had to be considered. The employer's failure to inform or consult did not help the employee, however, because only the kind of drastic action he took could have saved the business. She lost her claim accordingly.

In *Gorictree* v. *Jenkinson* (1984) the E.A.T. was at pains to reconsider the rigours of earlier interpretations, and reached a different conclusion. The tribunal observed that redundancy was one of the most common of all the economic, technical or organisational reasons for dismissal to which Regulation 8 applied. If these reasons were in fact to include redundancy they would deprive employees of an important existing statutory right. The tribunal thought that very clear words would be needed to bring about that result, and held that the words used in the Regulations did not satisfy that requirement. In the case in hand, the new employer dismissed his employees to make way for self-employed workers. That was undoubtedly a redundancy situation, and so despite the take-over the tribunal held them entitled to redundancy pay. In any event, said the tribunal, Regulation 8 applied only to Part V of the 1978 Act, which concerns unfair dismissals, and not to Part VI, which regulates redundancies. It appears therefore that the Regulations do not affect a new employer's liability for redundancy pay, nor alternatively for unfair dismissal if the surrounding circumstances are unfair: *McGrath* v. *Rank* (1985).

We note also that the expression 'changes in the workforce' means changes in the personnel employed and not merely changes in their terms and conditions. So where new owners of a company reduced an employee's wages in order to bring them into line with their own existing employees' rates, it was held both that the Regulations did not apply because other personnel were not affected, and also that cutting wages amounted to constructive dismissal: *Delabole* v. *Berriman* (1985).

Lastly in this connection, transferor and transferee employers should observe the duty cast upon them by the Regulations to give any recognised union details of the proposed takeover and consult on changes likely to affect members. Employees (union members or otherwise) may be awarded up to two weeks' pay if an employer fails in this duty. Further rules as to consultation are mentioned below.

7.13　(7) Calculation of redundancy pay

Assuming the requisite continuity of service, as explained in [7.10] above, redundancy payments are calculated in accordance with Schedule 4 of the 1978 Act. A maximum of twenty years' service is taken into account and gross earnings over £155 a week (the figure set for 1986–7) are disregarded. Within these limits, the rates are half a week's pay for each year of service between the ages of eighteen and twenty-one; one week's pay for each year of service between twenty-two and forty; and one and a half week's pay for each year between forty-one and the employee's last birthday before retirement. Since redundancy money is not payable on retirement, payment is reduced by one twelfth for every month of work after a man's sixty-fourth or a woman's fifty-ninth birthday. The current maximum payment is therefore £155 × $1\frac{1}{2}$ × 20 = £4650, though average payments are substantially less. The sum is tax-free and does not affect entitlement to unemployment benefit. Payment should be made on the day notice expires or the contract comes to an end, and any claim for it must be made within six months of that date if reasonably practicable. A written statement must also be given showing how the sum has been calculated, or otherwise it may be regarded as an *ex gratia* payment which would not affect the employee's statutory rights.

If the employer has calculated his liability correctly he can recover a proportion of his payment from the National Redundancy Fund administered by the Department of Employment. Except for small firms with fewer than ten employees, this entitlement is to be ended for redundancies taking effect after 31 October 1986. The Department will pay the redundant employee if the employer cannot, and then become the employer's creditor. If an employee dies after dismissal his claim passes to his personal representative.

Difficulties may arise in determining an employee's weekly pay – the basis of the calculation. The rules are laid down in Schedule 14. The weekly pay of a 'time' worker – one whose pay in his normal (i.e. contractually binding) hours does not vary with the amount of work done – is whatever is due to him under his contract for his normal hours. For anyone else – piece workers, shift workers and others whose hours are not fixed or whose rates vary with the day or hour – an average weekly rate is reached by adding up all the hours worked in the twelve working weeks before dismissal and dividing the result by twelve. Overtime hours are included in this calculation, but are deemed paid for at standard rate. Since overtime hours are not usually contractually binding they are not otherwise taken into account, however long and regularly overtime may in fact be worked and however unavoidable it may be in practice: *Lotus* v. *Sutcliffe* (1982). Weekly pay includes commissions and bonuses to which the employee is entitled and payments in kind which are part of his remuneration, such as accommodation: *R* v. *Leeds C.C.* (1983). Expense allowances, however, are excluded.

Final points on payment are that employers can avoid or reduce their statutory obligations where employees are entitled to pensions before retirement age. The pension or lump sum must be more than a mere return of contributions, and must become payable within ninety weeks of dismissal. Redundancy pay can only be avoided altogether if the annual value of the pension is at least one third of the employee's annual pay. Payment may also be reduced or refused if an employee is guilty of misconduct or goes on strike after he has been given notice for redundancy: *Simmonds* v. *Hoover* (1975).

7.14 Notification and consultation

Last but certainly not least we should note the various collective bargaining and administrative requirements involved in redundancy which are imposed by the Employment Protection Act 1975. Section 99 of this Act obliges employers to consult with officials of recognised unions (below) before declaring large-scale redundancies at any one 'establishment'. An establishment usually occupies one site only, but may sometimes be interpreted as 'the enterprise', e.g. where a building company occupies several different sites. Specifically, where an employer proposes to make one hundred or more employees redundant at an establishment within ninety days he must consult the union at least ninety days before the first dismissal takes effect (i.e. before the employee leaves), and where ten or more are to be dismissed within thirty days he must consult at least thirty days beforehand. No minimum period is laid down where fewer than ten employees are affected, but by inference it should be long enough to be useful. Written notice must also be given to the Department of Employment. Consultation with the union must begin before individual employees are given notice. It involves a written statement of the reasons for dismissal, the numbers and descriptions of the employees in question and the total number of such employees at that establishment, the proposed method of selection and dates of dismissal. The employer must then consider union representations and give a reasoned reply if he rejects them.

If an employer fails to consult as required the union can ask the tribunal for a 'protective award'. The employer's only defence is that of 'special circumstances' making consultation impracticable – which does not apply merely because of likely loss of morale or financial loss, unless disastrous: *U.S.D.A.W.* v. *Leancut Bacon* (1981). Even insolvency is not of itself a special circumstance: *Jowett* v. *N.U.T.G.W.* (1985). Protective awards are enforceable by the employees concerned. They oblige the employer to go on paying the wages of those who have been or will be dismissed for up to three months, depending on the numbers involved, the losses suffered by the employees and the gravity of the employer's failure to comply: *Spillers French* v. *U.S.D.A.W.* (1979). An employee fairly dismissed while the award is in force loses his entitlement under it, as do those who unreasonably end their contracts or refuse re-employment. Failure to notify the Department of Employment may result in the employer losing up to one tenth of his redundancy rebate and a fine not exceeding £400.

7.15 Union recognition

A union's right to consultation over redundancy depends on whether it is recognised. But how and when does an employer recognise a union? Difficulties may arise without an express agreement. In the leading case of *N.U.G.S.A.T.* v. *Albury* (1978), the Court of Appeal stressed that recognition was a most important matter for the industry concerned and so clear agreement on the issue was necessary, whether express or implied. In this case the employer belonged to a federation which negotiated with the union, but he himself had not previously employed union members and the union could not establish more than a little correspondence and one unsuccessful meeting between them. On the facts there was no recognition. Similarly, in *T.G.W.U.* v. *Courtenham* (1977) the fact that on one occasion a union official had represented a worker did not amount to recognition. A right to represent employees is different from and less significant than the right to negotiate on their behalf. Agreement to discuss redundancies constituted recognition in *U.S.D.A.W.* v. *Sketchley* (1981) as did periodic discussions on general terms and conditions of employment in *N.U.T.G.W.* v. *Ingram* (1977).

It may be helpful finally to remind employers very briefly of the miscellaneous further consequences of union recognition. As noted earlier, there is a duty to notify union representatives of impending take-overs and mergers and to discuss their 'legal, economic and social implications'. Officials of recognised unions must be given reasonable time off with pay for industrial relations work and training. Safety representatives are similarly entitled. Union members have a right to reasonable time off (not necessarily with pay) to take part in union activities. And overall an employer who recognises a union is bound to provide it with all the information reasonably required for the purposes of meaningful collective bargaining.

Chapter 8

Preparing and Presenting Cases at Tribunals

8.01 The claim

We assume now that a dismissal has taken place. The employer no doubt believes that he had good reason and acted fairly throughout – but this does not affect the likelihood or otherwise of the employee claiming against him. It could be said that employees have nothing to lose in this situation, and certainly if they are union members the union usually advises them to sue and undertakes to represent them whatever the merits of their case. Some employers cannot face the resulting 'hassle'. They are acutely aware of the time and effort needed to prepare their defence and in particular the costs incurred when half a dozen shop floor and management witnesses have to spend a day or two or even more at the hearing. They will be troubled by lingering doubts as to the outcome of the case, doubts inherent in all legal proceedings. On balance they may find it easier and more economical to buy off the applicant's claim by offering £100 or £200 without prejudice and in full settlement.

This course of action is not necessarily wrong; indeed the calculation may be a very realistic one. We can only say that the proper response to a claim should depend on the strength of the employer's defence. If he believes he acted rightly and has a couple of reliable witnesses he may do himself a disservice by settling. There is often more at stake than the rights and wrongs of the incident which led to dismissal. Basic standards of honesty or care may have to be asserted or the fundamental issue of the employer's right to manage resolved. If it was necessary to dismiss in the first place it is probably equally necessary to stand by that decision when the challenge comes.

The challenge is made when the employer receives a copy of form IT1 (Figs 8.1 and 8.2). The form is available at any employment office or unemployment benefit office and requires a simple statement of circumstances of the applicant's case against the respondent employer – or he may write a letter if he prefers. The employee will not be penalised by asking for the wrong remedy, e.g. compensation for unfair dismissal when his entitlement is to redundancy pay. The form or letter is sent to the Central Office of Industrial Tribunals at 93 Ebury Bridge Road, London SW1; 141 West Nile Street, Glasgow; or Bedford House, Bedford Street, Belfast. The Central Office sends a copy to the Regional Office which sends a copy to the respondent employer with an explanatory letter, form IT2, and another copy to ACAS (or, in Northern Ireland, the Labour Relations Agency).

8.02 Time limits

Claims must be received by the Central Office within three months of the 'effective date of termination' of the contract, or six months in redundancy cases, unless it was 'not reasonably practicable' to claim within the time limit: section 67 of the Employment Protection (Consolidation) Act 1978. Much depends, therefore, on establishing the exact date of termination. Section 55 says that if notice is given, employment ends the day notice expires, whether or not the employee is required to work out his notice. The period of notice must be at least that which the employee is entitled to by law: see [3.02]. If the employee wishes to leave before notice expires he may give a counter-notice, in which case the 'effective date' is the day he leaves.

Where the contract is ended summarily, i.e. without notice, or with money in lieu, employment ends on the last day of work. We should note, however, that this rule applies only for the purposes of deciding when a claim must be brought, and not for deciding whether an employee has served for the requisite two years. An employee dismissed without notice just before the end of his first two years may still have a claim, because section 55 of the Act enables him to add his statutory entitlement to notice onto the time

ORIGINATING APPLICATION TO AN INDUSTRIAL TRIBUNAL

IMPORTANT: DO NOT FILL IN THIS FORM UNTIL YOU HAVE READ THE NOTES FOR GUIDANCE. THEN COMPLETE ITEMS 1, 2, 4 AND 12 AND ALL OTHER ITEMS RELEVANT TO YOUR CASE, AND SEND THE FORM TO THE FOLLOWING ADDRESS

For Official Use Only	
Case Number	

To: THE SECRETARY OF THE TRIBUNALS
CENTRAL OFFICE OF THE INDUSTRIAL TRIBUNALS
(ENGLAND AND WALES)
93 EBURY BRIDGE ROAD, LONDON SW1W 8RE
Telephone: 01 730 9161

1   I hereby apply for a decision of a Tribunal on the following question. (STATE HERE THE QUESTION TO BE DECIDED BY A TRIBUNAL. EXPLAIN THE GROUNDS OVERLEAF).

....

2   My name is (Mr/Mrs/Miss   Surname in block capitals first):-

....

My address is:- ....

....

....Telephone No. ....

My date of birth is ....

3   If a representative has agreed to act for you in this case please give his or her name and address below and note that further communications will be sent to your representative and not to you *(See Note 4)*

Name of Representative:- ....

Address:- ....

....Telephone No. ....,..........

4   (a) Name of respondent(s) (in block capitals) ie the employer, person or body against whom a decision is sought *(See Note 3)*

....

Address(es) ....

....   Telephone No. ....

(b)   Respondent's relationship to you for the purpose of the application (eg) employer, trade union, employment agency, employer recognising the union making application, etc). ....

....

Fig. 8.1. Form IT1: employee's application.

5 Place of employment to which this application relates, or place where act complained about took place.

....

6 My occupation or position held/applied for, or other relationship to the respondent named above (eg user of a service supplied in relation to employment) ....

7 Dates employment began ....and (*if appropriate*) ended ......

8 (a) Basic wages/salary ....

   (b) Average take home pay ....

9 Other remuneration or benefits ....

10 Normal basic weekly hours of work ....

11 (In an application under the Sex Discrimination Act or the Race Relations Act)
   Date on which action complained of took place or first came to my knowledge ....

Please continue overleaf

12 You are required to set out the grounds for your application below, giving full particulars of them.

13 If you wish to state what in your opinion was the reason for your dismissal, please do so here.

14 If the Tribunal decides that you were unfairly dismissed, please state which of the following you would prefer: reinstatement, re-engagement or compensation. (Before answering this question please consult the leaflet "Dismissal – Employees' Rights", or, "Unfairly Dismissed?"

....

   Signature ....Date ....
IT1 (**Revised September 1979**)

FOR OFFICIAL USE ONLY

Received at COIT	Code	ROIT	Inits

Fig. 8.2. Form IT1: reverse side.

actually served. Alternatively, he has – as we saw in Chapter 2 – a claim for damages for wrongful dismissal, which may include compensation for loss of protection against unfair dismissal: *Cort* v. *Charman* (1981).

For employees on fixed term contracts, the effective date of termination is the day the term expires without renewal. When an employee resigns and claims constructive dismissal, the effective date is the day he leaves – whether or not he gives notice.

A surprisingly large number of claims fall outside the three-month limit. Employees then have to persuade the tribunals that it was 'not reasonably practicable' for them to claim in time – a phrase which has been narrowly interpreted. It has been held, for example, that no extension of time will be granted to an applicant who knows – or as a reasonably informed citizen or union member ought to know – that he can seek compensation, unless actually prevented from claiming because of illness or other events beyond his control such as postal delays: *Beanstalk Shelving* v. *Horn* (1980). The applicant may misunderstand the precise nature of his rights or details of the time limit but is still usually expected to claim in time. Exceptionally, and perhaps anomalously, in *Wall's* v. *Kahn* (1978), a claimant's reasonable belief that unfair dismissal proceedings would be settled in the course of his claim for unemployment pay was regarded as sufficient justification for delay. The strict general rule remains applicable even though the misunderstanding may have arisen through bad advice from a lawyer (in which case the disappointed applicant may sue his lawyer for professional negligence). But if the claimant has been wrongly advised by someone who could not necessarily be expected to know the law, or if some particular aspect of the law is in doubt, more time may be allowed: *Dedman* v. *British Building* (1974). A Citizen's Advice Bureau or full-time union official should know the law: *Riley* v. *Tesco* (1980). In *Norgett* v. *Luton Co-operative Society* (1976), the court refused to accept that an applicant's anxiety to have other legal proceedings resolved first – such as a criminal charge arising out of the incident for which he was dismissed – could be a valid reason for delay. Similarly, in *Palmer* v. *Southend B.C.* (1984) the Court of Appeal held that pursuit of a domestic appeal procedure did not of itself affect the reasonable practicability of making a claim in time.

8.03   The reply

Having received the claim, should the employer put the conduct of the case in the hands of a solicitor? The solicitor can advise what to say in answer, what evidence is needed, what letters or other documents are required from the other side, and eventually will put the employer's case before the tribunal, undertaking what should be for him the familiar task of examining witnesses and relieving the employer accordingly of a great deal of worry. Alternatively, he may brief a barrister to do all these things. Lawyers are used in perhaps one third of all contested cases, more often by employers than employees, and figures suggest that they improve the chances of winning by some 4 or 5 per cent. For these advantages an employer might expect to pay his representative perhaps £150-200 a day in the provinces and twice as much in London. Fees might be substantially greater if there is much preliminary work to be done or 'City' firms are used. They must be paid by the employer whether he wins or loses.

Only the employer can decide whether such expenditure is warranted. He might reflect, however, that because it is a relatively new subject many solicitors are unfamiliar with the rules of labour law and the procedure and requirements of industrial tribunals. The lawyer necessarily knows less about the facts of the case than management representatives, and may alienate the tribunal by unnecessary legalism. Tribunal procedure is deliberately designed to be straightforward and not to need legal skills. And in any case most disputes concern simply questions of fact – as to who said what, where and to whom – which do not require court-room skills of cross-examination and should be within the competence of any manager to resolve. A personnel officer should, in fact, be more than capable of handling the whole issue himself from start to finish, unless he can see, with the general legal knowledge he ought to have, that a difficult question of law is involved and legal assistance is desirable. If the other side decides to employ a lawyer that should not of itself affect his judgment.

Let us suppose it is company policy to leave dismissal in the hands of the personnel officer or his equivalent, and that it is his job to ensure that dismissal policies are laid down and followed in line with the ACAS Code (see Chapter 6). When he receives form IT1,

INDUSTRIAL TRIBUNALS

NOTICE OF APPEARANCE BY RESPONDENT   Case Number _____

To the Assistant Secretary of Tribunals

                                           FOR OFFICIAL USE

                                           Date of receipt   Initials

1.   I*do/do not intend to resist the claim made by _____

2.   *My/Our name is *Mr/Mrs/Miss/Title (if a company or organisation):-

     Name: _____

     Address: _____

                _____   Telephone Number

                _____   _____

3.   If a representative is acting for you, please give his/her name and address
     and note that all further communications will be sent to him/her, not to you:

     Name: _____

     Address: _____

                _____   Telephone Number

                _____   _____

4.   (a)   Was the applicant dismissed?   *YES/NO

     (b)   If YES, what was the reason for dismissal?

     (c)   Are the dates given by the applicant as to the period of employment
           correct?   *YES/NO

     (d)   If NO, give dates of commencement _____ and termination _____

     (e)   Are details of remuneration stated by the applicant correct? *YES/NO

     (f)   If NO, or if the applicant has not stated such details, please give the
           correct details:-

           Basic Wages/Salary: _____

           Average take home pay: _____

           Other remuneration or benefits: _____

*Delete inappropriate items   Please continue overleaf

Fig. 8.3. Form IT3: employer's response.

(g)   (To be completed <u>only</u> when the application relates to Maternity Rights)
When the applicant's absence began were you employing more than 5
persons?   *YES/NO

(h)   (To be completed in other applications)

   (i)   When the applicant's employment ended were you employing more
than 20 persons?   *YES/NO

   (ii)   If NO, had you at anytime during the applicant's employment with
you employed more than 20 persons?   *YES/NO.

5.   If the claim is resisted, you should give below sufficient particulars to
show the grounds on which you intend to resist the application.

(Continue on a separate sheet if there is insufficient space below).

Signature ....   Date ....

IT3 (Revised August 1981)   * Delete inappropriate terms

212/9/9

Fig. 8.4. Form IT3: reverse side.

or a letter to the same effect, he should reply on form IT3 (Figs 8.3 and 8.4). This 'notice of appearance' requires him to outline in ordinary language the circumstances of the case and management's reason or reasons for dismissal. Simple examples might be: 'The applicant was a foreman in the respondent's stores. At about 10.30 am on 4 April 1986 he was seen to leave the stores carrying two widgets each worth £100 without having signed for them. He was interviewed on 7 April but could give no explanation. He was therefore dismissed for gross misconduct.' Or again: 'The applicant was employed as a shop assistant. She was between five minutes and half an hour late on some fifteen occasions in the three months before dismissal. She had previously been warned against lateness and during these three months received two further warnings. After her last warning on 4 April 1986 she was ten minutes late on 8 April and half an hour late on 10 April. She was dismissed on that day for gross misconduct or other substantial reason.' It will be seen that the vital facts are shortly but sufficiently recorded and all inessential details omitted.

Effectively the same explanation should be given directly to the employee if he exercises his right under section 53 of the 1978 Act to require a written statement of the reasons for his dismissal. This right arises after six months' service. The employer can meet the demand by referring him to some previous written explanation such as a letter of dismissal. Either way the applicant should be adequately informed of the employer's reasons, and if the statement is inadequate (e.g. says simply 'misconduct') or inaccurate, or is not provided within fourteen days of the request (unless it is not reasonably practicable to provide it), the applicant is entitled to two weeks' pay. Any marked divergence between this statement and the employer's reply on form IT3 will obviously be very damaging to the employer.

Tribunals are not much concerned with the 'label' the employer gives to his reason for dismissal. What he has called misconduct, for example, they may regard as incapacity or some other substantial reason. So long as they are satisfied that the reason he gives is the real reason, it will be upheld if it is any one of the five good reasons accepted by the 1978 Act. As indicated above, therefore, employers may give alternative labels if they wish. On the other hand, tribunals cannot substitute reasons which were not given merely because they think they are better reasons, nor can the employer purport to dismiss for one reason and then advance an entirely different one, even on the same facts, to the tribunal. This latter point is illustrated in *Hotson* v. *Wisbech Conservative Club* (1984) where the employee was told she was dismissed on grounds of inefficiency but on the same facts was accused at the tribunal of dishonesty. Her dismissal was held unfair because this was a quite different complaint to have to answer without warning.

8.04   Conciliation

Once the nature of the claim and defence have become clear the employer may expect a visit from a conciliation officer employed by the Advisory, Conciliation and Arbitration Service. The officer's duty is laid down by section 134 of the 1978 Act. At the request of both sides, or of his own volition if he thinks he has a reasonable chance of success, he must try to promote a settlement between the parties and so avoid altogether the need for a tribunal hearing. In the first place he will seek the complainant's reinstatement or re-engagement on whatever terms seem fair, or failing that, agreement as to compensation.

The conciliation officer's position is open to misunderstanding and accusations of bias and pressure are occasionally made against him. In fact, his role is essentially that of an independent and impartial go-between. He is there to seek common ground; not to advise, and still less to bring pressure to bear on one side or the other. But if asked, no doubt he would offer an opinion on the merits of the case or a proposed settlement, and his opinion should be a very helpful guide.

Tribunals will not interfere with the way the officer does his job nor with settlements he helps to bring about, unless they have evidence of bad faith or fundamental error. On principle any written or oral settlement reached with his approval is final: *Gilbert* v. *Kembridge* (1984). Employers should note that this is not true of settlements which are not reached through ACAS. Even if stated to be final they may not prevent the employee from bringing a claim because he cannot be deprived of his statutory rights by contract.

Conciliation in dismissal cases is widely accepted and evidently mutually agreeable in the sense that some two-thirds of claims made every year are settled in this way, with consequent savings in time and worry. Payments are made in about half these cases. In 1983 the median amount was £421. As we said earlier, however, there are still many cases where the employer has no conceivable reason to settle and so in due course the parties make their way to the tribunal.

8.05   Statements and documents

Taking witnesses' statements is a vital step in preparing a case. The personnel officer should confirm that written statements taken before dismissal are still adequate, and if not take new ones. As the date of the hearing draws nearer he should give his witnesses copies of what they have said and go over these again with them.

It may be difficult to decide how many witnesses to call. Four or five may have seen the same incident and would say the same thing. Should they all be called? Is it necessary to call a person who signed a letter, or is it sufficient simply to produce the letter? Employers do not want to give the impression of taking a sledgehammer to crack a nut, nor to waste their own employees' valuable time, but the fact remains that several witnesses are better than one, particularly where there are flat conflicts of evidence between the two sides on crucial issues. Whether the writers of letters and reports etc. need to be called depends on the importance of the letters. If they record decisions directly affecting the applicant it is not just a matter of calling a witness to vouch for his own signature but to explain the decisions.

In general, spoken evidence of facts within a witness's knowledge is preferable to hearsay evidence – which is what someone said who is not before the court – and very much more convincing than written evidence. But if a witness cannot be or does not wish to be called – for example, because of illness, or because he is no longer or never has been an employee (see *Khanum* v. *Mid Glamorgan A.H.A.* [6.03]) – or if there is no dispute as to the content of the letter or report, the tribunal should accept written matter at its face value. As a last resort the tribunal can be asked for a witness order to compel attendance, though involuntary witnesses may not be very helpful. In deciding what evidence to bring and what form it should take the personnel officer can do no better than put himself in the position of the tribunal and ask what he would want to know in that capacity. And in case of doubt it is always better to be safe than sorry.

Copies of all relevant documents should be collected. These may include the original job advertisement, letters of application and acceptance, the job description, other terms of employment required to be in writing [1.04-1.05], disciplinary rules, union agreements, records of interviews and warnings, pay slips and the like. If dismissal on grounds of race or sex is alleged, appropriate employment records will be called for. Both sides should try to agree on the documentary evidence they will need, which may involve exchange of documents. If the personnel officer has no copy of an essential letter or document which he believes is in the applicant's possession, he should ask the applicant for a copy and if it is not provided should apply to the Regional Office of Industrial Tribunals for an order for discovery or inspection of documents. His application to the Regional Office should include a copy of his original request and a short statement of his reasons for wanting to see the document. A fine is payable if the tribunal's order is disobeyed. Any additional document must be disclosed if those already disclosed would be misleading without it: *Bird's Eye* v. *Harrison* (1985).

Ideally, then, both sides will agree on a common bundle of documents, usually in chronological order and numbered accordingly (and if sufficiently bulky and complex, provided with a contents list), which is of the greatest assistance to the tribunal. Apart from the personnel officer's own copy, copies of any given document should be available for each of the three members of the tribunal, the other side's representative and the witness who is to vouch for the document or be questioned on it as the case may be.

Any fear of defaming someone through public disclosure of these documents can be discounted. Statements made in courts and tribunals are protected by absolute privilege, i.e. they cannot be sued upon unless unrelated to the case in hand. Statements becoming available before trial by exchange of documents are probably covered by qualified privilege, and so cannot be regarded as defamatory even though untrue and harmful – unless made with knowledge of their untruth and with intent to injure.

8.06 At the tribunal

The tribunal hearing usually takes place between one and three months after the employer has returned form IT3. The date is notified on form IT4 (Fig. 8.5). It is fixed without consultation with the parties and sometimes with only a couple of weeks' notice. This may be very inconvenient – perhaps a key witness is going on holiday, or one's legal representative, if any, is not available. A letter to the tribunal clerk and thence the chairman is then necessary, explaining the circumstances and asking for postponement. Most tribunals are willing to help, but not all. It is a matter for the chairman's discretion, and some abuse their position by arbitrary refusal to cooperate. Regrettably, no appeal can be made against such abuse of office.

Before the main hearing, either side may ask for a 'pre-hearing assessment', or the tribunal itself may order one. The purpose is to confirm that there are genuine grounds for making or defending a claim, or that the claim is within the tribunal's jurisdiction (as where, for example, the tribunal is asked to give a remedy for breach of contract or wrongful dismissal, or an opinion on the rights and wrongs of a situation – none of which are within its power). These assessments may involve oral arguments or written submissions, but no witnesses. The tribunal then gives its written opinion, and if it finds one side's case without merit will warn that party that if he continues the fight and loses before another tribunal he may have to pay the other side's costs. Another possibility is a 'preliminary hearing', at which arguments as to the applicant's length of service or other such qualifying right are decided. The respondent employer may raise objections of this kind in his IT3, or the tribunal may take the point itself.

Assuming that the case reaches full hearing, the personnel officer should be at the tribunal office on the appointed day with his witnesses at least half an hour before the normal 10.00 am start.

THE INDUSTRIAL TRIBUNALS

NOTICE OF HEARING

Case No ....

NOTICE IS HEREBY GIVEN THAT THE application of
has been listed for hearing by an Industrial Tribunal at:-

on   day,   19   at   am/pm

1.   Attendance should be at the above time and place. The parties (other than a
respondent who has not entered an appearance) are entitled to appear at the
hearing and to state their case in person or be represented by anyone they wish.
A party can choose not to appear and can rely on written representations (which if
additional to any already submitted must be sent to the Tribunal and copied to the
other party not less than 7 days before the hearing). However, experience shows
that it is normally advisable for a party and any witnesses to attend in person
even if they have made statements or representations in writing.

2.   It is very important that each party should bring to the hearing any
documents that may be relevant, eg a letter of appointment, contract of
employment, Working Rule Agreement, pay slips, income tax forms, evidence of
unemployment and other social security benefits, wages book, details of benefits
and contributions under any pension or superannuation scheme, etc.

3.   If the complaint is one of unfair dismissal or refusal of permission for a
woman employee to return to work after a pregnancy the tribunal may wish to
consider whether to make an order for reinstatement or re-engagement. In these
cases the respondent should be prepared to give evidence at the hearing as to the
availability of the job from which the applicant was dismissed, or held before
absence due to pregnancy, or of comparable or suitable employment and generally as
to the practicability of reinstatement or re-engagement of the applicant by the
respondent.

4.   If for any reason a party (other than a respondent who has not entered an
appearance) does not propose to appear at the hearing, either personally or by
representative, he should inform me immediately, in writing, giving the reason and
the case number. He should also state whether he wishes the hearing to proceed in
his absence, relying on any written representations he may have made. If an
applicant fails to appear at the hearing the tribunal may dismiss or dispose of
the application in his absence.

5.   The hearing of this case will take place at the time stated above or as soon
thereafter as the tribunal can hear it.

To the Applicant(s) (Ref   )   Signed ....
                                        for Assistant Secretary of the Tribunals

                                        Date ....

                                  ┌───┐
                                  │ NOTE Representatives who receive this   │
                                  │ notice must inform the party they   │
and the Respondent(s) (Ref   )│ represent of the date, time and place of │
                                  │ the hearing. The party will not be   │
                                  │ notified direct.   │
                                  └───┘

IT4
(Nov 78)   *Fig. 8.5.* Form IT4: notice of hearing.

He will be asked first to give a clerk his and his witnesses' names and addresses and to provide a list of any cases he may wish to cite. He should then spend the next half hour taking his witnesses once more through their written statements, setting fears or nerves at rest, and reminding them how to give evidence. The most important point is to explain that although he or the other side's representative will ask the questions, witnesses' answers *must not be addressed back to the questioner but to the members of the tribunal*. He should also stress that they should speak slowly and keep their voices up, and not say more than they are asked. Facilities for these briefings are usually poor, but the Central Office at Ebury Bridge Road in London is a most commendable exception with separate rooms for applicants and respondents, and refreshments are also available.

Tribunal members are a solicitor or barrister as full-time or part-time chairman or chairwoman and two 'wingmen' – laymen or women nominated respectively by the CBI and TUC. Although nominated on this 'partisan' basis they are not there to represent one interest against the other. Their job is to provide practical experience and advice for the chairman and in reaching judgment to correct any tendency to excessive legalism. Decisions are on a majority basis.

The composition of tribunals has been questioned; trade unionists sometimes regard them as representing a built-in two-to-one majority against them, which might seem to suggest that the only fair tribunal would be one consisting of three trade unionists. It is nonetheless true that certain lawyer-chairmen or women appear sometimes to forget the essentially down-to-earth nature of the proceedings. They seem to imagine themselves in court, free to bully witnesses or nit-pick over the admissibility of evidence, or obliged as judges to take down in laborious long-hand every word the witnesses utter, apparently incapable of distinguishing between the significant and the trivial, or to take over the questioning of witnesses and in one way or another prolong the proceedings far beyond their proper span. The conduct of a case may, in short, depend to a surprising extent upon their idiosyncracies, and no doubt their training in this respect could be improved.

8.07   The hearing

Tribunal cases are almost always heard in public. The Regulations recognise that exceptional circumstances might occur which justify or necessitate secrecy, but these are confined to questions of national security or where it would be illegal or in breach of confidence to disclose information, or where disclosure would cause substantial damage to the employer's undertaking. A private hearing will not be granted merely because of possible embarrassment or unpleasantness.

The case begins. In constructive dismissal cases [3.09-3.10] it is for the employee to show first that he was indeed dismissed. Normally, however, the burden of proof is upon the employer, and so the proceedings begin with the chairman asking the employer's representative whether he wants to make an opening statement or call his witnesses immediately. In Scotland the practice is not to make a statement, but both there and in England and Wales the tribunal can decide its own procedure.

We shall suppose that the personnel officer – or lawyer, as appropriate – wishes to outline the case. He remains seated and speaks to the chairman or chairwoman, addressing him or her as 'Sir' or 'Ma'am'. He will briefly draw the tribunal's attention to any particular point of law he needs to establish – for which he will bring textbooks or case reports – and then equally shortly summarise the facts and the part played by each witness. He may offer the tribunal his bundle of documents at that stage but in any case will have to ask the relevant witness to vouch for each document in turn. It is helpful to admit at the outset any difficulty he may face in proving his case, such as absence of written warnings or records of absenteeism, and explain how he proposes to overcome the problem.

The employer's representative then calls his witnesses, usually in the chronological order in which they became involved in the case. After the witness is sworn in, the representative asks his or her name and occupation, and then takes the witness through his or her statement. Questions should be short and simple, and the chairman given time to write down the answer if he wishes before another question is asked. Personnel officers or other lay representatives are not expected to act like lawyers, but should appreciate the uses and misuses of leading questions. A leading question can be defined as one which contains or suggests an answer, e.g. 'At lunch-time were you in the canteen?' as distinct from the 'open' question: 'Where were you at lunch-time?' Leading a witness is a convenient and acceptable way of speeding up the proceedings and bringing him to the point at issue, but should not be pursued when that point is reached. The tribunal will not be impressed by witnesses who cannot give an account of the vital facts without having words put into their mouths.

When the witness has told his story it is the turn of the employee or his representative to cross-examine him – if possible to prove his recollection at fault and to see what he thinks about the employee's version of events. Leading questions are permissible throughout cross-examination. If the employee is not represented he will probably find questioning quite difficult and will tend simply to make statements contradicting management's witnesses. The chairman will then ask the witness to say whether or not he agrees with these assertions. The personnel officer should be sure to write down any of his witness's answers which seem to depart from his original account, and he can examine on these if he so wishes. After his re-examination the tribunal members may ask questions, and both sides are usually allowed to pursue any new issues raised at that point.

After each of the employer's witnesses has been examined, cross-examined and re-examined it is now the employee's turn. He and his witnesses go through the same sequence of events, questioned first by their own representative, usually a shop steward, and then cross-examined by the personnel officer and finally re-examined by their own representative. Tribunal procedure does not require either side to tell the other who will be called as witnesses nor what they will say, so there is always the possibility of surprise at this stage. If completely unexpected arguments or allegations are put forward the personnel officer can ask for an adjournment to consider the position, or seek to recall a witness.

When the last witness has been heard the applicant or his representative makes a final speech , summing up the weaknesses of the employer's witnesses and the strength and consistency of his own, stressing perhaps the burden of proof, an unblemished record and matters of that kind. The personnel officer then makes his final speech. This should be short and to the point, stressing briefly the integrity of his own witnesses and the fallibility of the other side's, the importance of preventing dishonesty or reducing absenteeism, or whatever was the cause of dismissal, and reminding the tribunal of the relevant rules of law.

We have said that personnel officers are not likely to be involved in arguing complex questions of law. It is normally sufficient simply to outline the twin requirements of good reason for dismissal and due observance of procedure, perhaps with a reference to the line of cases which require only that dismissal be within the band of reasonable responses of a reasonable employer: see [3.12]. But even for this purpose it will be seen that personnel officers should know the relevant sections of the 1978 Act and be ready if need be to cite a Court of Appeal or Employment Appeal Tribunal case or two in their favour. Other cases at industrial tribunal level are not binding on tribunals even though their facts may appear similar, and so are of little value unless some significant proposition of law can be found in them.

8.08 The decision

Depending, as we have said, on the idiosyncracies of the chairman, most cases should not last for more than one day. If time allows after a short case there will be an adjournment and an hour or two later the chairman will announce the tribunal's decision. But more probably the decision will be sent by post within the following month or so; certainly in those cases which last several days. In Chapter 9 we deal with the questions of compensation which will arise if the decision goes against the employer.

Tribunal judgments used to set out the facts in great detail, sometimes adding lengthy legal arguments, before reaching their conclusions. After changes introduced by the Industrial Tribunals (Rules of Procedure) Regulations 1985, they are now generally much shorter, stating only the factual basis for the decision. But the parties may still ask for a detailed decision, or it may in any case be given if an appeal seems likely. The Employment Appeal Tribunal can ask the tribunal to amplify its findings and reasons.

8.09 Review and appeal

Notes accompanying the decision tell the parties that they may seek a 'review' within fourteen days thereafter. The tribunal can review, i.e. reconsider, its decision if the judgment shows some clear and important factual error, or if vital new evidence has emerged, or a party inadvertently missed the original hearing and has been penalised accordingly, or more generally if 'the interests of justice' so require. In practice reviews are rare.

The notes also advise the parties of their right to appeal to the Employment Appeal Tribunal at 4 St. James's Square, London SW1 or 249 West George Street, Glasgow, within forty-two days of the date of registration of the judgment, which is the day it is sent out. Appeals to the Employment Appeal Tribunal do not involve rehearing the case or re-examining witnesses. They can only be made on questions of law – though it is not always easy to say exactly what that means. Nearly all dismissal cases involve a decision on what is fair. Is fairness a question of law? The overall answer must be 'no'. The Employment Appeal Tribunal has said many times that each case turns on its own facts and that it cannot and will not interfere with tribunals' holdings on particular sets of facts.

But if it can be argued that a decision was 'perverse' – that 'no reasonable tribunal' could reach such a decision, then that is a question of law on which an appeal can be made. It will be seen that this requires much more than a difference of opinion over the decision. In effect, the argument is that the tribunal has completely misunderstood or failed to take account of the facts or the law or has otherwise behaved quite irrationally. A very heavy burden of proof thus rests upon the appellant, and successful appeals are correspondingly few. A further appeal on a question of law can be made to the Court of Appeal. Legal advice and representation is highly desirable if an appeal is contemplated, though still not essential. Employees may be assisted here by the Legal Aid Fund, which is not available at industrial tribunal level. Free legal advice on the conduct of industrial tribunal claims may, however, be available – depending on the employee's income.

Chapter 9

Liability

9.01 Employees' remedies

We have noted that only about one third of each year's dismissal claims reach tribunal hearings, the rest being settled or withdrawn, and that employees formally win only about one tenth of the total number of claims. That still represents some 3000 or so cases each year in which employers have failed to make the elementary inquiries or take the other precautions described in previous chapters, and so are found to have acted arbitrarily and unjustly. This final chapter deals with the results of that conclusion.

The Employment Protection (Consolidation) Act 1978 enables tribunals to order reinstatement, re-engagement or compensation. It is clear from the terms of sections 68-71 of the Act that so far as the law is concerned reinstatement or re-engagement orders are the primary remedies, much preferred to money in lieu. In practice, however, these orders are given very rarely – in only about 3 per cent of the successful claims.

9.02 Reinstatement and re-engagement

On holding an employer liable for unfair dismissal the tribunal must tell the applicant that his reinstatement or re-engagement can be ordered if it is practicable in the circumstances. If he wants one or other of these remedies the tribunal may make whichever order is appropriate, or at its discretion award compensation instead. A reinstatement order obliges the employer to give back to the applicant all the rights and privileges of his former employment together with any benefits he would otherwise have received from it, and states how much he must be paid for the time lost from work. This sum depends on the applicant's earnings in other employment or his social security payments. A re-engagement order may require the applicant to be taken back in his old job on new terms, perhaps with loss of seniority, or given other suitable work with his former employer or an associated employer. The type of work, rate of pay, rights and privileges, starting date and amount due in the meantime, if any, must be specified in the order.

It will be seen that the decision to make a reinstatement or re-engagement order depends first upon the applicant's wishes and second upon practicability. Applicants do not always ask for an order, perhaps having found other work elsewhere or because they realise the relationship has been damaged beyond repair. If they do ask they are likely to be refused if to any great extent to blame for their dismissal, or if the employer can convince the tribunal he would be justified in refusing to obey an order – for example, because of poor relationships between the applicant and other employees or serious allegations of bad faith made during the tribunal hearing. Grounds such as these clearly make reinstatement impracticable. Tribunals have no power to settle a case on the understanding that the employer will offer re-employment, and this way of resolving disputes is discouraged.

When considering whether to make an order the tribunal must disregard the fact that the employer has appointed someone else to do the applicant's work – unless persuaded that the employer had no alternative, or that he did not know the applicant sought re-employment and had to have a permanent replacement for him.

9.03 Additional award

The penalty for disobeying a reinstatement or re-engagement order is laid down in section 71 of the Act and is in the form of an additional award to the employee. Additional awards are usually the equivalent of thirteen to twenty-six weeks' pay, but will be between twenty-six and fifty-two weeks' pay if dismissal arises out of union membership or race or sex discrimination. Earnings over £155 per week (1986-7 rates) are disregarded, and so the maximum award under section 71 is currently £8060. The practicability or otherwise of reinstatement or re-engagement should not be finally decided until the employee returns to the tribunal claiming that the employer has failed to comply with an order. An additional award must not be made if it could be fulfilled only by dismissal of another employee: *Freemans* v. *Flynn* (1984).

COMPENSATION

9.04 (1) Basic award

In nearly every case, however, unfair dismissal is dealt with by an award of compensation, calculated under sections 72-4 of the Act. Awards are classified as basic and compensatory. Basic awards are calculated in the same way as redundancy payments (see Chapter 8) and in fact represent applicants' accrued rights to redundancy pay. Since they are not strictly redundancy payments, however, no part of them can be recovered by the employer from the Department of Employment. The maximum basic award in 1986-7 is £4650. Not less than £2200 must be awarded to applicants unfairly dimissed for refusing to join a closed shop, as to which see also the special award, below. If the cause of the unfair dismissal is redundancy but the employee is not entitled to redundancy pay because he has unreasonably refused re-employment, the basic award is two weeks' pay: section 73(2).

9.05 (2) Compensatory award

This part of the award is intended to cover the economic losses the applicant has suffered or is likely to suffer because of dismissal, so far as such losses can be estimated within the few months following dismissal. Because economic loss alone can be compensated, the manner or indignity of dismissal or degree of unfairness involved is not relevant: *Morris* v. *Acco* (1985). The burden of proving his loss is upon the applicant, and the tribunal is directed by section 74 of the 1978 Act to award whatever compensation seems 'just and equitable', within the present statutory limit of £8000.

The precise amount awarded depends essentially on the difference in pay between the old job and the new, or between the old job and unemployment as the case may be. When measuring loss of salary prospects the tribunal must see how long it would take the applicant to reach his former rate of pay and award him the net shortfall for the resulting number of months or years: *Tradewinds* v. *Fletcher* (1981). If by finding a better job elsewhere he suffers no loss he is not entitled to compensation.

Specific items in the calculation include loss of perks such as tips, use of a car, and loss of rights to notice and protection against unfair dismissal for the following two years. Pension rights are very important. Guidance is given to tribunals by a document prepared by the Government Actuary's Department, but it is accepted that the calculation of pension rights will be a rough and ready one. The tribunal will not require the applicant to produce his own actuarial or statistical evidence, and if the employer cares to do so that will be at his expense and risk: *Manpower* v. *Hearne* (1983). Loss of tax rebates is taken into account, but no deduction made for minor rebates: *Lucas* v. *Scott* (1983): *M.B.S.* v. *Calo* (1983). If the applicant was dismissed without notice, pay in lieu or earnings or social security benefit received during the proper period of notice should be disregarded: *T.B.A.* v. *Locke* (1984). Any *ex gratia* payment by the employer should be deducted from the total sum to which the employee appears entitled before the statutory limit is applied: *McCarthy* v. *B.I.C.C.* (1985). If by the date of hearing the applicant had found other employment but lost it again because of redundancy his resulting unemployment is the responsibility of the second employer, not the first: *Courtaulds* v. *Moosa* (1984).

Tribunals do not directly deduct unemployment pay from their awards, but tell employers not to pay that part of the award representing current loss of earnings until the Department of Employment decides whether to issue a recoupment notice. If a notice is issued the employer pays to the Department a sum equivalent to the applicant's unemployment pay, and what is left of his wages to the applicant.

Both basic and compensatory awards may be substantially reduced if the applicant is partly to blame for his own misfortunes or if dismissal would otherwise have been inevitable. Management is entitled to argue that any procedural or other failures on its part which make dismissal unfair should be offset by the employee's misconduct or incapacity or other unacceptable activities such as unreasonable wage demands: *Dobson* v. *Morritt* (1972). Refusal to join or take part in the activities of a union is not blameworthy conduct.

Evidence of misconduct etc. which comes to light only after dismissal cannot be used to justify dismissal (contrary to the rule in wrongful dismissal: Chapter 2), but may certainly reduce the compensation payable and perhaps even negate it altogether. 'Parliament cannot possibly have intended that a dishonest employee who has successfully concealed his defalcations up to the time of dismissal, whose conduct, if known, would justify his summary dismissal, should, in addition to the proceeds of his dishonesty, obtain compensation from his employers': *Devis* v. *Atkins* (1977). Evidence of imminent redundancy is likewise admissible to reduce compensation.

Compensation will also be reduced if the applicant does not take reasonable steps after dismissal to minimise his losses by, for example, accepting a satisfactory offer of re-employment or, in particular, by seeking other suitable work elsewhere. Management might find it helpful to keep records of employment opportunities in their area. Depending on his needs and circumstances, however, a dismissed employee is not always bound to accept work which would pay less than unemployment benefit. Applicants should not be penalised for trying to set up in business on their own account. On the other hand, an applicant who starts on a training course after dismissal is deemed to take himself off the labour market at that time and his compensation is reduced accordingly. An employee's refusal to pursue in-house rights of appeal is not a ground for reducing compensation. When reductions are justified they are commonly of the order of 30 or even 50 per cent or more.

As a general rule, the employer cannot escape liability for dismissal by showing that he was forced to dismiss by threats of industrial action. Compensation is assessed 'as if no such pressure had been exercised': section 74(5). But in the exceptional case of industrial action or threat of action intended to bring about an employee's dismissal because he is not a member of a union, the employer or complainant can ask the tribunal to bring in the person making the threats as a party to the proceedings. Such a request must be granted if made before the hearing begins but may be refused thereafter. If this unlawful form of pressure is proved the tribunal can order the wrongdoer, in practice the union, to pay the whole or any part of the award: section 76A.

9.06   Special award

Employees dismissed for joining or refusing to join a union, and who have asked unsuccessfully for reinstatement or re-employment, are entitled to a special award. Under section 75A the award is between £11,000 and £22,000 (1986/7) where the tribunal declines to order reinstatement or re-engagement and not less than £16,500 if such an order is made but not obeyed. Reductions may be made if the employee's conduct contributed to his dismissal, or if he prevented or rejected re-employment. Bearing in mind the procedure under section 76A above and the likelihood of union liability we can see that the primary purpose of the special award is to deter unions from forcing the dismissal of employees lawfully entitled not to join closed shops.

9.07   Miscellaneous issues: costs

We recall here briefly certain other liabilities arising out of dismissal which have been noted in earlier chapters. Employees dismissed after six months' service are entitled to ask for a written statement of the reasons for dismissal. A penalty of two weeks' pay is imposed for unreasonable failure to comply within fourteen days of such a request. Employees alleging dismissal because of union membership or non-membership can apply to the tribunal for interim orders preserving their contractual rights until the issue is resolved.

If an employer becomes insolvent and cannot pay an award the Department of Employment pays the employee the basic award and becomes the employer's creditor for that amount. On the same grounds, the Department will also pay wages due during statutory periods of notice, up to the 1986/7 maximum of £155 per week. In other cases of failure to pay an award, the complainant may begin an action in the county court or, in Scotland, the Sheriff Court. Claims may be made to tribunals or courts on behalf of employees who die after dismissal. Interest is due on unpaid awards.

Usually each side bears its own costs, win or lose, though witnesses' costs are reimbursed out of public funds, within statutory limits. But the tribunal can order one side to pay the other's costs or part of them if its conduct of the case was frivolous or vexatious, e.g. because serious but totally unfounded accusations were made or because at the last moment the claim or defence was abandoned. Costs can also be ordered against a party who has ignored the advice given him in a pre-hearing assessment: see [8.06].

9.08 Conclusion

No one will ever be completely satisfied with the way the law works, but from the employer's point of view at least there seems little to complain of in this particular context. He will no doubt accept that the days of arbitrary dismissal of long-serving employees, with all the resulting hardship and ill-will, are rightly over. In almost every case, the onus of proving the fairness of dismissal is imposed directly upon the employer, and he may have to pay considerable sums if he fails. But we have seen that the burden is not a very heavy one. It is really no more than that which any reasonable employer would think right and proper – that of treating each case on its merits and each employee with the respect he deserves.

Industrial Tribunal Addresses

Central Office of the Industrial Tribunals (England and Wales)

93 Ebury Bridge Road
London SW1W 8RE
Tel: 01-730 9161

Regional Offices of the Industrial Tribunals (England and Wales)

Birmingham

Regional Office
Phoenix House
1–3 Newhall Street
Birmingham B3 3NH
Tel: 021-236 6051

Office of the Industrial Tribunals
22/23 Mardol
Shrewsbury, SY1 1PU
Tel: 0743-58341

Bristol

Regional Office
Prince House
43/51 Prince Street
Bristol BS1 4PE
Tel: 0272-298261

Office of the Industrial Tribunals
Renslade House
Bonhay Road
Exeter EX4 3BX
Tel: 0392-79665

Bury St Edmunds
Regional Office
Southgate Street
Bury St Edmunds
Suffolk IP33 2AQ
Tel: 0284-62171

Offices of the Industrial Tribunals
8/10 Howard Street
Bedford, MK40 2HS
Tel: 0234-51306

Sussex House
Hobson Street
Cambridge CB1 1NL
Tel: 0223-311331

Cardiff
Regional Office
Caradog House
1–6 St Andrews Place
Cardiff CF1 3BE
Tel: 0222-372693

Leeds
Regional Office
Minerva House
East Parade
Leeds LS1 5JZ
Tel: 0532-459741

Office of the Industrial Tribunals
2nd Floor
Strand House
Beverley Road
Hull HU3 1SA
Tel: 0482-20433

Liverpool
Regional Office
No. 1 Union Court
Cork Street
Liverpool L2 4UJ
Tel: 051-236 9397

London (Central)
Regional Office
93 Ebury Bridge Road
London SW1W 8RE
Tel: 01-730 9161

Office of the Industrial Tribunals
Tufton House
Tufton Street
Ashford
Kent TN23 1RJ
Tel: 0233-21346

London (North)
Regional Office
19/29 Woburn Place
London WC1H 0LU
Tel: 01-632 4921

London (South)

Regional Office
93 Ebury Bridge Road
London SW1W 8RE
Tel: 01-730 9161

Office of the Industrial Tribunals
49 Buckingham Place
Brighton BN1 3PQ
Tel: 0273-24402

Manchester
Regional Office
Alexandra House
14–22 The Parsonage
Manchester M3 2JA
Tel: 061-833 0581

Newcastle-upon-Tyne

Regional Office
Plummer House (3rd Floor)
Market Street East
Newcastle-upon-Tyne
NE1 6NF
Tel: 0632-328865/7

Office of the Industrial Tribunals
12–16 Woodlands Road
Middlesbrough
Cleveland TS1 3BE
Tel: 0642-249437/8

Nottingham

Regional Office
7th Floor
Birkbeck House
Trinity Square
Nottingham
Tel: 0602-45701

Office of the Industrial Tribunals
31–33 Millstone Lane
Leicester
Tel: 0533-530119

Sheffield
Regional Office
14 East Parade
Sheffield S1 2ET
Tel: 0742-760348

Southampton

Regional Office
Duke's Keep
(3rd Floor)
Marsh Lane
Southampton SO1 1EX
Tel: 0703-39555

Office of the Industrial Tribunals
30–31 Friar Street
Reading RG1 1DY
Tel: 0734-594917/9

Central Office of the Industrial Tribunals (Scotland)
St Andrew House
141 West Nile Street
Glasgow G1 2RU
Tel: 041-331 1601

Edinburgh
Office of the Industrial Tribunals
124/125 Princes Street
Edinburgh EH2 4AD
Tel: 031-226 5584

Dundee
Office of the Industrial Tribunals
2nd Floor
13 Albert Square
Dundee
DD1 1DD
Tel: 0382-21578

Aberdeen
Office of the Industrial Tribunals
252 Union Street
Aberdeen AB1 1TN
Tel: 0224-643307

**Central Office of the Industrial Tribunals
(Northern Ireland)**

Bedford House
Bedford Street
Belfast
Tel: 0232-227666

ACAS Code of Practice 1: Disciplinary Practice and Procedures in Employment

This Code is issued pursuant to section 6(1) and (8) of the Employment Protection Act 1975 and comes into effect, by order of the Secretary of State, on 20 June, 1977.´

A failure on the part of any person to observe any provision of a Code of Practice shall not itself render him liable to any proceedings; but in any proceedings before an industrial tribunal or the Central Arbitration Committee any Code of Practice issued under this section shall be admissible in evidence, and if any provision of such a Code appears to the tribunal or Committee to be relevant to any question arising in the proceedings it shall be taken into account in determining that question. (Employment Protection Act 1975 section 6(11).)

Introduction

This Code supersedes paragraphs 130 to 133 (inclusive) of the Code of Practice in effect under Part I of Schedule I to the Trade Union and Labour Relations Act 1974, which paragraphs shall cease to have effect on the date on which this Code comes into effect.

1 This document gives practical guidance on how to draw up disciplinary rules and procedures and how to operate them effectively. Its aim is to help employers and trade unions as well as individual employees—both men and women— wherever they are employed regardless of the size of the organisation in which they work. In the smaller establishments it may not be practicable to adopt all the detailed provisions, but most of the features listed in paragraph 10 could be adopted and incorporated into a simple procedure.

Why have disciplinary rules and procedures?

2 Disciplinary rules and procedures are necessary for promoting fairness and order in the treatment of individuals and in the conduct of industrial relations. They also assist an organisation to operate effectively. Rules set standards of conduct at work ; procedure helps to ensure that the standards are adhered to and also provides a fair method of dealing with alleged failures to observe them.

3 It is important that employees know what standards of conduct are expected of them and the Contracts of Employment Act 1972 (as amended by the Employment Protection Act 1975) requires employers to provide written information for their employees about certain aspects of their disciplinary rules and procedures.*

4 The importance of disciplinary rules and procedures has also been recognised by the law relating to dismissals, since the grounds for

---

*Contracts of Employment Act 1972 S.4(2) as amended by Employment Protection Act Schedule 16 Part II requires employers to provide employees with a written statement of the main terms and conditions of their employment. Such statements must also specify any disciplinary rules applicable to them and indicate the person to whom they should apply if they are dissatisfied with any disciplinary decision. The statement should explain any further steps which exist in any procedure for dealing with disciplinary decisions or grievances. The employer may satisfy these requirements by referring the employees to a reasonably accessible document which provides the necessary information.

dismissal and the way in which the dismissal has been handled can be challenged before an industrial tribunal.* Where either of these is found by a tribunal to have been unfair the employer may be ordered to reinstate or re-engage the employees concerned and may be liable to pay compensation to them.

Formulating policy

5　　Management is responsible for maintaining discipline within the organisation and for ensuring that there are adequate disciplinary rules and procedures. The initiative for establishing these will normally lie with management. However, if they are to be fully effective the rules and procedures need to be accepted as reasonable both by those who are to be covered by them and by those who operate them. Management should therefore aim to secure the involvement of employees and all levels of management when formulating new or revising existing rules and procedures. In the light of particular circumstances in different companies and industries trade union officials** may or may not wish to participate in the formulation of the rules but they should participate fully with management in agreeing the procedural arrangements which will apply to their members and in seeing that these arrangements are used consistently and fairly.

Rules

6　　It is unlikely that any set of disciplinary rules can cover all circumstances that may arise : moreover the rules required will vary according to particular circumstances such as the type of work, working conditions and size of establishment. When drawing up rules the aim should be to specify clearly and concisely those necessary for the efficient and safe performance of work and for the maintenance of satisfactory relations within the workforce and between employees and management. Rules should not be so general as to be meaningless.

7　　Rules should be readily available and management should make every effort to ensure that employees know and understand them. This may be best achieved by giving every employee a copy of the rules and by

---

*The Trade Union and Labour Relations Act 1974 Schedule I para 21(4), as amended by the Employment Protection Act 1975 Schedule 16 Part III specifies that a complaint of unfair dismissal has to be presented to an Industrial Tribunal before the end of the 3-month period beginning with the effective date of termination.

**Throughout this Code, trade union official has the meaning assigned to it by S.30(1) of the Trade Union and Labour Relations Act 1974 and means, broadly, officers of the union, its branches and sections, and anyone else, including fellow employees, appointed or elected under the union's rules to represent members.

explaining them orally. In the case of new employees this should form part of an induction programme.

8 Employees should be made aware of the likely consequences of breaking rules and in particular they should be given a clear indication of the type of conduct which may warrant summary dismissal.

Essential features of disciplinary procedures

9 Disciplinary procedures should not be viewed primarily as a means of imposing sanctions. They should also be designed to emphasise and encourage improvements in individual conduct.

10 Disciplinary procedures should :
(a) Be in writing.
(b) Specify to whom they apply.
(c) Provide for matters to be dealt with quickly.
(d) Indicate the disciplinary actions which may be taken.
(e) Specify the levels of management which have the authority to take the various forms of disciplinary action, ensuring that immediate superiors do not normally have the power to dismiss without reference to senior management.
(f) Provide for individuals to be informed of the complaints against them and to be given an opportunity to state their case before decisions are reached.
(g) Give individuals the right to be accompanied by a trade union representative or by a fellow employee of their choice.
(h) Ensure that, except for gross misconduct, no employees are dismissed for a first breach of discipline.
(i) Ensure that disciplinary action is not taken until the case has been carefully investigated.
(j) Ensure that individuals are given an explanation for any penalty imposed.
(k) Provide a right of appeal and specify the procedure to be followed.

The procedure in operation

11 When a disciplinary matter arises, the supervisor or manager should first establish the facts promptly before recollections fade, taking into account the statements of any available witnesses. In serious cases consideration should be given to a brief period of suspension while the case is investigated and this suspension should be with pay. Before a decision is made or penalty imposed the individual should be interviewed and given the opportunity to state his or her case and should be advised of any rights under the procedure, including the right to be accompanied.

12   Often supervisors will give informal oral warnings for the purpose of improving conduct when employees commit minor infringements of the established standards of conduct. However, where the facts of a case appear to call for disciplinary action, other than summary dismissal, the following procedure should normally be observed:

(a) In the case of minor offences the individual should be given a formal oral warning or if the issue is more serious, there should be a written warning setting out the nature of the offence and the likely consequences of further offences. In either case the individual should be advised that the warning constitutes the first formal stage of the procedure.

(b) Further misconduct might warrant a final written warning which should contain a statement that any recurrence would lead to suspension or dismissal or some other penalty, as the case may be.

(c) The final step might be disciplinary transfer, or disciplinary suspension without pay (but only if these are allowed for by an express or implied condition of the contract of employment), or dismissal, according to the nature of the misconduct. Special consideration should be given before imposing disciplinary suspension without pay and it should not normally be for a prolonged period.

13   Except in the event of an oral warning, details of any disciplinary action should be given in writing to the employee and if desired, to his or her representative. At the same time the employee should be told of any right of appeal, how to make it and to whom.

14   When determining the disciplinary action to be taken the supervisor or manager should bear in mind the need to satisfy the test of reasonableness in all the circumstances. So far as possible, account should be taken of the employee's record and any other relevant factors.

15   Special consideration should be given to the way in which disciplinary procedures are to operate in exceptional cases. For example:

(a) **Employees to whom the full procedure is not immediately available.** Special provisions may have to be made for the handling of disciplinary matters among nightshift workers, workers in isolated locations or depots or others who may pose particular problems for example because no one is present with the necessary authority to take disciplinary action or no trade union representative is immediately available.

(b) **Trade union officials.** Disciplinary action against a trade union official can lead to a serious dispute if it is seen as an attack on the union's functions. Although normal disciplinary standards should apply to their conduct as employees, no disciplinary action beyond an oral warning should be taken until the circumstances of the case have been discussed with a senior trade union representative or full-time official.

(c) **Criminal offences outside employment.** These should not be treated as automatic reasons for dismissal regardless of whether the offence has any relevance to the duties of the individual as an employee. The main considerations should be whether the offence is one that makes the individual unsuitable for his or her type of work or unacceptable to other employees. Employees should not be dismissed solely because a charge against them is pending or because they are absent through having been remanded in custody.

Appeals

16   Grievance procedures are sometimes used for dealing with disciplinary appeals though it is normally more appropriate to keep the two kinds of procedure separate since the disciplinary issues are in general best resolved within the organisation and need to be dealt with more speedily than others. The external stages of a grievance procedure may however, be the appropriate machinery for dealing with appeals against disciplinary action where a final decision within the organisation is contested or where the matter becomes a collective issue between management and a trade union.

17   Independent arbitration is sometimes an appropriate means of resolving disciplinary issues. Where the parties concerned agree, it may constitute the final stage of procedure.

Records

18   Records should be kept, detailing the nature of any breach of disciplinary rules, the action taken and the reasons for it, whether an appeal was lodged, its outcome and any subsequent developments. These records should be carefully safeguarded and kept confidential.

19   Except in agreed special circumstances breaches of disciplinary rules should be disregarded after a specified period of satisfactory conduct.

Further action

20   Rules and procedures should be reviewed periodically in the light of any developments in employment legislation or industrial relations practice and, if necessary, revised in order to ensure their continuing relevance and effectiveness. Any amendments and additional rules imposing new obligations should be introduced only after reasonable notice has been given to all employees and, where appropriate, their representatives have been informed.

Draft Revision of ACAS Code of Practice: Disciplinary and Other Procedures in Employment

Note: The present draft is intended to replace the Code of Practice on Disciplinary Practice and Procedures in Employment brought into effect on 20 June 1977 (see Appendix 2) and paragraphs 44–46 of the earlier Industrial Relations Code of Practice brought into effect on 28 February 1972. This draft was issued by ACAS for consultation and comment in November 1985.

INTRODUCTION

1.   This Code gives practical guidance on how to draw up rules and procedures about employment and how to operate them effectively.   Its aim is to help employers and trade unions as well as individual employees wherever they are employed and regardless of the size of the organisation in which they work. In smaller establishments it may not be practicable to adopt all the detailed provisions set out here.   Nonetheless in every organisation there should be clearly understood procedures,   however simple,   which are consistent with the general principles and intentions of this Code.

2.   The Code is concerned not only with discipline but also other procedural matters which may present difficulties for both employers and employees.   It is in five parts.   Part 1 gives general guidance on the need for rules and procedures and the other parts set out procedures on discipline,   absence, sub-standard work and redundancy handling.   Proper procedures are an aid to good management and should not be viewed primarily as a means of imposing sanctions or as necessarily leading to dismissal.   The aim is to ensure that employees are treated fairly and consistently and that,   where an employee's job is at risk,   proper and adequate procedures are observed before any

decision is taken to dismiss. The correct application of procedures should benefit both employers and employees and may in practice lead to fewer dismissals and disagreements about them.

3. The guidance set out does not relieve an employer of responsibility for looking carefully at every case and trying to reach a fair and reasonable decision. Neither does it restrict an employer from taking whatever course of action is judged appropriate according to the circumstances of a particular case.

PART ONE: THE NEED FOR RULES AND PROCEDURES

4. Rules and procedures are necessary for promoting fairness and consistency in the treatment of individuals and in the conduct of industrial relations. They also assist an organisation to operate effectively. There is a difference between them. Rules set standards of conduct at work; procedures help to ensure that the standards are adhered to and also provide a fair method of dealing with alleged failures to observe them.

5. The importance of rules and procedures has been particularly recognised in the law relating to dismissals, since in certain circumstances the grounds for dismissal and the way in which the dismissal has been handled may be challenged before an industrial tribunal. Where, for either of these reasons, the tribunal finds the dismissal unfair the employer may be ordered to reinstate or re-engage the employee concerned or may be liable to pay compensation. Where, in the view of the tribunal, the employer refuses unreasonably to comply with an order to reinstate or re-engage the tribunal may make an additional award of compensation. In coming to a decision about the fairness or otherwise of a dismissal, the tribunal will have regard not only to the existence of and adherence to any procedure in operation but also to whether the employer acted reasonably in all the circumstances.

Formulating Rules and Procedures

6. The initiative for establishing adequate rules and procedures will normally lie with management. To be fully effective the rules and procedures need to be accepted as reasonable both by those who are to be covered by them and those who operate them. Management should aim to secure the involvement of employees and all levels of management when formulating new or revising existing rules and procedures. Where a trade union is recognised by the

employer, trade union officials[*] may or may not wish to participate in the formulation of rules but may see advantages in participating fully with management in agreeing the procedural arrangements which will apply to their members and in seeing that these arrangements are used consistently and fairly.

Rules

7.   It is unlikely that any set of rules can cover all situations that may arise: moreover the rules required will vary according to particular circumstances such as the type of work,   working conditions and size of establishment.   In drawing up, communicating and applying rules the following guidance should be borne in mind:-

o   rules should be specified clearly and unambiguously and should apply to all employees

o   rules should generally be written down and accessible to all employees

o   in the case of new employees,   an explanation of rules should form part of the induction process[**]

o   rules should set out any conditions attaching to probationary periods both at the commencement of employment and on promotion

o   special attention should be paid to communicating rules to young persons with little or no previous experience of working life

----

[*]   Throughout this Code, trade union officials has the meaning assigned to it by S30(1) of the Trade Union and Labour Relations Act 1974 and means, broadly, officers of the union, its branches and sections, and anyone else, including fellow employees, appointed or elected under the union's rules to represent members.

[**]   The Employment Protection (Consolidation) Act 1978 S1 requires employers to provide employees with a written statement of the main terms and conditions of their employment covering pay, hours of work, holidays, incapacity for work due to sickness or injury, pensions and pension schemes, notice and job title.   The employer may satisfy these requirements by referring the employees to a reasonably accessible document which provides the necessary information.

o   where the workforce includes employees whose English is limited, it may be necessary for rules to be translated

o   where rules form part of a collective agreement, management should ensure in liaison with trade union officials that they are communicated to employees concerned

o   rules should be applied consistently

o   where a rule has fallen into disuse, employees should be advised before the rule is re-introduced or there is any change in what has previously been the practice.

Revision of Rules and Procedures

8.   From time to time rules and procedures should be reviewed in the light of developments in employment legislation, industrial relations practice, technological change and the changing needs of the organisation to ensure that they continue to be effective and relevant. Some conditions e.g. those which form part of the contract of employment may need re-negotiation. The unreasonable imposition of amended rules without agreement may adversely affect industrial relations. Additional or amended rules imposing new obligations · should be introduced only after employees and their representatives have been consulted and an opportunity given for discussion of the proposed changes. Any changes should be communicated to employees in advance of the changes taking effect. This may be achieved by issuing an amendment to or an amended version of the written particulars of employment.

PART TWO: DISCIPLINARY PROCEDURES

9.   It is important that employees know what standards of conduct are expected of them and in support of this the Employment Protection (Consolidation) Act 1978 requires employers to provide written information for their employees about certain aspects of their disciplinary rules and procedures.[*]

----

[*]   The written information must specify any disciplinary rules applicable to employees and indicate the person to whom they should apply if they are dissatisfied with any disciplinary decision. The statement should explain any further steps which exist in any procedure for dealing with disciplinary decisions or grievances. The employer may satisfy these requirements by referring the employees to a reasonably accessible document which provides the necessary information.

10. Disciplinary procedures should:-

o   Be in writing

o   Specify to whom they apply

o   Provide for matters to be dealt with quickly

o   Indicate the disciplinary actions which may be taken

o   Specify the levels of management which have the authority to take
     the various forms of disciplinary action and ensure that immediate
     supervisors do not normally have the power to dismiss without
     reference to senior management

o   Provide for individuals to be informed of specific complaints
     against them and to be given an opportunity to state their case
     directly to those considering disciplinary action before decisions
     are reached

o   Give individuals the right to be accompanied, either by a trade
     union official where a trade union is recognised or by a fellow
     employee of their choice

o   Ensure that any investigatory period of suspension is with pay
     (unless the contract of employment clearly provides otherwise) and
     specify how pay is to be calculated during such a period

o   Ensure that, except for gross misconduct, no employees are dismissed
     for a first breach of discipline

o   Ensure that disciplinary action is not taken until the case has been
     carefully investigated

o   Ensure that individuals are given a written explanation for any
     penalty imposed

o   Provide a right of appeal and specify the procedure to be followed
     and the action which may be taken by those hearing the appeal.

Conduct justifying summary dismissal

11. Employees should be given a clear indication of the type of conduct which will normally warrant dismissal for a first time offence, without the normal period of notice or pay in lieu of notice. Some offences may appear to be minor in themselves but because of the nature of the employer's business considered serious enough to justify dismissal for a first offence. Offences which fall into this category must be clearly specified in the rules. If the list of offences to be treated as gross misconduct is not to be regarded as exhaustive, this should be stated in the rules.

Disciplinary Procedures: Informal Warnings

12. After establishing the facts, the supervisor may consider that there is no need to resort to the formal procedure and that it is sufficient to talk the matter over with the employee. Such discussion should normally take place out of the hearing of other employees unless it is operationally necessary to take action immediately. Supervisors should be clear as to the difference between an informal oral warning of this kind issued in the context of counselling and an oral warning issued as part of the formal procedure, and the recipient should be left in no doubt as to which sort of warning has been issued. Informal oral warnings should not be documented in the employee's personal record, although it may be advisable for a note to be kept by the supervisor for reference purposes.

13. Occasions on which informal oral warnings are given should not be allowed to escalate into disciplinary hearings as this may mean the employee is denied certain rights, such as the right to be accompanied. If the informal oral warning fails to resolve the matter, the discussion should be adjourned and the matter pursued under the formal disciplinary procedure.

14. Where the supervisor comes to the conclusion that disciplinary action is not appropriate, it should be made quite clear to the employee that no action is to be taken.

The Formal Procedure in Operation

15. When a disciplinary matter arises and it is considered that action beyond an informal oral warning is called for, the following procedure should normally apply:-

- the supervisor or manager should establish the facts promptly before memory fades, taking into account the statements of any available witnesses

- consideration should be given in serious cases to a brief period of suspension with pay while the case is investigated, unless the contract of employment provides for suspension without pay in such circumstances

- the employee should be interviewed, told what is being alleged against him or her, given a written statement of the allegation and advised of any rights under the procedure, including the right to be accompanied

- the employee should be given time to prepare and given an opportunity to state his or her case

- a decision as to what took place should be made before any decision is taken about disciplinary action

- if more time is needed to consider the matter or further investigations are necessary, the interview should be adjourned and resumed later.

Deciding The Disciplinary Action

16. Before deciding whether disciplinary action is appropriate and the form it should take, consideration should be given to the following:-

- the employee's disciplinary record and whether he or she is aware of the standards required

- the employee's age, position, length of service and general performance

- any circumstances, for example domestic problems, which make it appropriate to lessen the severity of the action

- whether the disciplinary procedure indicates what the likely action will be as a result of the particular misconduct

- the action taken in similar cases in the past

°   whether the proposed action is reasonable in all the circumstances

17. Where the facts of a case appear to call for disciplinary action, other than summary dismissal, the following procedure should normally be observed:-

°   in the case of minor offences the individual should be given a formal oral warning and should be advised that the warning constitutes the first formal stage of the procedure. A note of the oral warning should be kept for reference purposes.

°   in the case of more serious offences or where there is an accumulation of minor offences the individual should be given a written warning setting out the precise nature of the offence, the likely consequences of further offences and specifying, if appropriate, what improvement is required and over what period.

°   if serious misconduct persists consideration should first be given to imposing disciplinary action other than dismissal but only if this is provided for in the disciplinary procedure. Such action might include disciplinary transfer, disciplinary suspension without pay, demotion, loss of seniority or loss of increment. Special consideration should be given before imposing disciplinary suspension without pay and where imposed it should not normally be for a prolonged period. Any disciplinary action imposed should be reasonable in relation to the offence and the circumstances surrounding it.

°   in the case of further offences or a first instance of very serious misconduct the individual should be given a final written warning setting out the precise nature of the offence and containing a statement that any recurrence will lead to dismissal or whatever other penalty is considered appropriate.

°   if all previous stages have been observed the final step will be dismissal with the appropriate period of notice or payment in lieu of notice.

First and Final Warning

18. There may be occasions when misconduct is considered to be insufficiently serious to justify dismissal but sufficiently serious to warrant only one written warning, which in effect will be both first and final. To provide for

this eventuality the disciplinary procedure should indicate that the procedure can be implemented at any stage, according to the seriousness of the offence.

Implementing The Action

19. Except in the event of an oral warning, details of any disciplinary action should be given in writing to the employee and where appropriate to his or her trade union official or employee representative. A copy should be retained by the employer. In particular the written notification should:

    o   state the precise nature of the misconduct.

    o   state, if appropriate, the period of time given for improvement and the improvement which is expected.

    o   specify the disciplinary action being taken and, where appropriate, how long the action will last.

    o   indicate the likely consequences of further misconduct.

    o   inform the employee of the right of appeal, how it should be made and to whom.

Action in Particular Cases

20. Special consideration should be given to the way in which disciplinary procedures are to operate in particular cases. For example:-

    o   Employees to whom the full procedure is not immediately available.

    Special provisions may have to be made for the handling of disciplinary matters among nightshift workers, weekend or Sunday workers, workers in isolated locations or depots or others who may pose particular problems for example because no one is present with the necessary authority to take disciplinary action or no trade union official is immediately available.

    o   Trade union officials.

    Disciplinary action against a trade union official can lead to a serious dispute if it is seen as an attack on the union's function. Normal disciplinary standards should apply to officials' conduct as employees but no disciplinary action beyond an oral warning should normally be taken until the circumstances of the case have been discussed with a senior trade union representative or full-time official.

o   Criminal Offences - General

Special attention should be paid to situations involving employees who are alleged to have committed criminal offences whether connected with employment or not.   In dealing with such situations employers should decide whether sufficient information exists before taking any disciplinary action which they may consider appropriate. They are not expected to establish whether the employee committed the offence beyond all reasonable doubt but rather whether the employee committed the offence on the balance of probability.   Where a criminal charge has been preferred,   they are not obliged to wait until the outcome of the criminal case is known.

o   Criminal   offences   arising   from   or   having   a   bearing   on employment

In all cases the employee should be informed of the complaint, asked for an explanation and the circumstances investigated as fully as possible.   In cases of doubt all likely explanations for what happened should be considered.   Where the police are called in they should not be asked to conduct the disciplinary investigation on behalf of the employer,   nor to be present at the disciplinary interview.   Before any decision is taken about disciplinary action, reasonable grounds must be established for believing that the individual committed the particular offence.

o   Criminal offences unconnected with employment

These should not automatically be treated as reasons for dismissal regardless of whether the offence has any relevance to the duties of the individual as an employee.   The main considerations should be whether the offence is one that makes the individual unsuitable for his or her type of work or unacceptable to other employees. Employees should not be dismissed solely because a charge against them is pending or because they are absent through having been remanded in custody.   Where an employee is on bail pending a court hearing or an appeal and is still available for work,   any decision concerning dismissal should be postponed if practicable - bearing in mind any effects on the employer's business - until the outcome of the case or the appeal is known. Where a custodial sentence is imposed and the employee is not available for work, employers must be mindful of the need to act reasonably, in the light of the needs of the business, before deciding whether or not to dismiss.

Appeals Procedure

21. Employers should ensure that the procedure to be followed in making an appeal against disciplinary action is made known to all employees and that the appeals procedure is operated correctly.

22. In some organisations a general grievance procedure covering other matters is used for hearing appeals against disciplinary action. While this may work well in small firms or for appeals against less severe disciplinary actions, on the whole a separate appeals procedure is more satisfactory for most organisations.

23. Appeals procedures should:-

   o   specify any time-limit within which the appeal should be lodged

   o   provide for appeals to be dealt with speedily particularly those involving suspension without pay or dismissal

   o   wherever possible, provide for the appeal to be heard by an authority higher than that taking the disciplinary action

   o   wherever possible, provide for the appeal to be heard by a person who is not the direct manager of the person taking the diciplinary action

   o   spell out the action which may be taken by those hearing the appeal

   o   provide for any new evidence, arising during an adjournment of the appeal, to be put to the employee before any decision is taken on the disciplinary action.

24. While it is desirable that appeals should be dealt with speedily, there should be an opportunity for all sides to reflect on what has been said at the disciplinary hearing and for the employee to consider how best to present the

appeal. In particular the appeal should not proceed with undue haste in a way which might lead the employee to believe that objective consideration is not being given to his or her case.

25. The final stage of some procedures is reference to independent arbitration or to a joint management-union panel. Where a final decision within an organisation is contested, or where the matter becomes a collective issue between management and union, the external stage of a grievance or disputes procedure may provide a convenient method of resolving the issue. Consideration should be given to whether ACAS conciliation and arbitration might be used as a means of assisting the parties to an acceptable solution.

Preservation of Statutory Rights During Appeals Procedure

26. Subject to the satisfaction of certain conditions, employees who feel that they have been unfairly dismissed have a statutory right to make a complaint of unfair dismissal to an industrial tribunal. Such complaints must normally be received by the tribunal within the period of 3 months beginning with the employee's effective date of termination.

27. Steps should be taken to ensure that employees are not deprived of their statutory rights simply because of the time which may be needed to process an internal appeal. Any decision to dismiss should be communicated clearly to employees and there should be no doubt as to what constitutes the effective date of termination. Where, exceptionally, the operation of an internal appeals procedure in relation to a dismissal suggests that a decision will not be reached within 3 months of the effective date of termination, employees should consider whether to present an application to the industrial tribunal at the outset and ask that the case should not be set down for hearing until the outcome of the internal appeal is known. Employers should not regard this action as affecting the internal appeal in any way.

Records

28. Records should be kept, detailing the nature of any breach of disciplinary rules, the action taken and the reasons for it, the date action taken, whether an appeal was lodged, its outcome and any subsequent developments. These records should be carefully safeguarded and kept confidential.

29. Disciplinary action should not be allowed to count against an employee indefinitely. Except in special circumstances any disciplinary action taken

should be disregarded for disciplinary purposes after a specified period of satisfactory conduct. In many cases a period between 6 months and 12 months will be reasonable, while in others a different period will be more appropriate depending on the offence and the type of disciplinary action imposed.

Staff Training

30. Those responsible for enforcing disciplinary rules and procedures need training for the task. Senior management should ensure that managers and supervisors have a thorough knowledge of their disciplinary rules and procedures and in particular know how to prepare for and conduct a disciplinary interview.

PART THREE: PROCEDURES RELATING TO ABSENCE

31. This section of the Code sets out procedures for dealing with long-term and short-term absences. It does not contain guidance on acceptable levels of absence: these will vary depending upon the particular circumstances of the employment.

32. In order to monitor absence levels, adequate attendance records are necessary. These should show the duration of, and reason for, all spells of absence. In some circumstances employees may have reasonable and legitimate grounds for needing to be absent from work. Employers should ensure that procedures specify clearly the types of absence for which authorisation in advance is required.

33. In dealing with absence a distinction should be made between absence on grounds of incapacity and absence for reasons which may call for disciplinary action. However in all cases involving absence sufficient enquiry should be made to enable a decision to be reached. Proper investigation and consultation with the employee is essential. Before any decision is taken concerning dismissal employers should ask themselves whether they have considered all available options and must be mindful of the need to act reasonably in all the circumstances.

Long-Term Absence due to Illness

34. Where an employee is absent through long-term ill-health, the first requirement is to try to discover the employee's true medical position. The following procedure should normally apply:-

- the employee should be consulted regularly and an attempt made to establish the length of time he or she is expected to be away

- the employee should be allowed a reasonable period of time in which to recover

- where possible, arrangements should be made to minimise the effect of his or her absence through re-organisation or the engagement of temporary staff

- the employee's permission should be sought in appropriate cases to approach his or her doctor to establish the likely length of absence, whether there will be any residual incapacity and whether the employee might be suitable for any alternative work

- where there is any doubt about the nature of the incapacity or where medical guidance is needed about the type of work which the employee should avoid or to which he or she is best suited, the employee's permission should be sought to approach a company or occupational doctor for an independent medical report

- the employee should be kept fully informed if employment is at risk.

Action in Particular Cases

35. Special consideration should be given to action which may be needed in particular cases. For example:-

- where the employee is unable to work because of adverse medical reaction to workplace conditions, consideration should be given to whether alternative work is available

- where the employee is allergic to a particular product used in the work process, consideration should be given to whether the conditions causing the allergy can be alleviated

- where the employee's medical condition is a potential danger to or may disturb others, consideration should be given to whether close contact with other employees can be eliminated or minimised

- where the employee is mentally ill a patient and understanding approach will be required, especially if treatment is likely to take some time. Where effective consultation with the employee proves

difficult,   contact   should   be   maintained   with   relatives,   if
possible,in order to keep in touch with the employee's progress.

36.   Disciplinary warnings should not be given to an employee who is on
long-term sick absence since these imply that the employee is being asked to
improve or change his or her conduct.   What is required is a more personal,
caring approach to try to establish whether the employee's need for time to
recover his or her health is compatible with the employer's need for work to
be done.

37.   The time may eventually come when, having considered all the facts, the
employee's job can no longer be kept open and no suitable alternative work
either full-time or part-time is available.   In such cases the position should
be explained to the employee before any dismissal action is taken and the
employee should be given the period of notice to which he or she is entitled.

Frequent and Persistent Short-Term Absences

38.   Where an employee is frequently or persistently absent,   it should be
borne in mind that the reason for taking time off may be medical or have
nothing to do with illness. The following procedure should normally apply:-

- o   the absences should be investigated promptly in order to be fair to
   the employee and to minimise any repercussive effects on other
   employees

- o   the employee should be invited to give an explanation for his or
   her absences and to indicate any mitigating circumstances

- o   where absences arise from temporary domestic problems the likelihood
   of an improvement in attendance should be considered in deciding
   what action is appropriate

- o   where as a result of self-certified absences the employee has not
   seen his or her family doctor, the employee should be asked to
   consult his or her own doctor to ascertain whether medical treatment
   is necessary and to establish whether the underlying reason for
   absence is work-related

- o   where a doctor's certificate has been produced but there is doubt
   about the reason for absence, further investigation via a company or

occupational doctor may be necessary in order to establish the actual position

○ in all cases the employee should be warned of the likely consequences, including the possibility of dismissal, if there is no improvement in attendance and told what improvement is expected

○ if there is no improvement in attendance, the employee's age, length of service, performance, the likelihood of a change in conduct, the availability of suitable alternative work and the effect the absences have had on the business should all be taken into account in deciding what action to take

○ any action taken should be consistent with the employer's current practice.

Other Absences

39. Employers may have policies which allow employees extended leave of absence to visit relatives in their countries of origin or relatives who have emigrated to other countries. In addition some employers may wish to allow employees extended leave for other special circumstances e.g. to nurse a sick relative. There is no statutory right to extended leave and whether it is granted is a matter for agreement between employers and their employees, or where appropriate, their trade unions.

40. Where a policy on extended leave is in operation, the following procedure will normally be appropriate:-

○ the arrangements for extended leave should be incorporated in the information on terms and conditions of employment given to all employees at the time employment commences

○ the policy should apply to all employees, irrespective of their ethnic origin

○ any conditions attaching to extended leave should be carefully explained to the employee and the employee's signature obtained as an acknowledgement that he or she understands and accepts the terms on which the leave is granted

○ interpreters should be used in appropriate cases

     o   the policy should specify the acceptability or otherwise of foreign medical certificates

     o   the policy should contain a clear statement of the consequences of any failure to return on the agreed date.

41. If an employee fails to return on the agreed date, the circumstances should be investigated as fully as possible and an effort made to contact the employee. Before any decision is taken because an employee has overstayed a period of extended leave, the employee's age, length of service, reliability record and any mitigating circumstances should all be taken into account. The need to act reasonably in all the circumstances should also be borne in mind.

Summary of Action in Absence Cases

42. There are various reasons for absence and they cannot all be covered in a Code of this kind. Nevertheless, in all types of case, the principles set out in this section of the Code apply before any action is taken to dismiss an employee who is absent from his or her place of work. In short, these are as follows:-

     o   a full investigation into the circumstances surrounding the absence

     o   an opportunity for the employee to state his or her case and to be accompanied, where appropriate, by a trade union official or fellow employee of his or her choice

     o   the issue of warnings and time for improvement where appropriate

     o   consideration of suitable alternative employment

     o   the need to act reasonably in all the circumstances.

PART FOUR: PROCEDURES RELATING TO SUB-STANDARD WORK

43. This section of the Code provides guidance on ways of minimising poor performance and a procedure for dealing with it should it occur.

Action Prior to Employment

44. Before employment begins consideration should be given to any steps which may need to be taken to minimise the risk of poor performance and to create

conditions which allow employees to carry out their duties satisfactorily. Careful recruitment, selection and induction procedures are essential and it is particularly important that job descriptions reflect accurately the main purpose and scope of each job and the tasks involved.

Action When Employment Begins

45. The following guidelines should be observed at the commencement of employment:-

   ° where probation periods are set employees should be made aware of the conditions which attach to them

   . ° the standard of work required should be explained orally during the induction programme and employees left in no doubt about the standards expected of them

   ° the consequences of any failure to meet the required standards should be fully explained

   ° any targets set should be realistic.

Action During Employment

46. Proper training, supervision and encouragement are essential to the achievement of satisfactory performance. During the course of employment performance should be appraised regularly and often, either formally or informally. Inadequate performance, particularly during probation periods, should be identified as soon as possible, so that appropriate remedial action can be taken.

47. Where a formal appraisal system is in operation, the assessment criteria should be examined to ensure that they are not discriminatory on grounds of race, colour, nationality, ethnic or national origins, sex or marriage.

48. In dealing with sub-standard work, negligence should be distinguished from incompetence. Negligence normally involves a measure of personal blame for which some form of action under the disciplinary procedure will be appropriate. In such cases the employee's ability will normally have been proved but his or her work subsequently found to be inadequate due to lack of motivation or attention. Incompetence, on the other hand, is due to lack of ability, skill or experience and may point to poor recruitment procedures,

inadequate training or inaccurate job descriptions. In cases where incompetence is alleged, consideration should be given to whether the situation might be improved by training or transfer to alternative work, rather than by taking disciplinary action.

49. Unsatisfactory performance may occur in employees whose skills, while relevant at the outset of employment, have become outmoded by new technology, re-organisation or changing patterns of work. Employers should act reasonably towards such employees and, where practicable, help them to achieve any new skills which may be required. If the primary cause of diminished performance is the changing nature of the job, consideration should be given to treating the situation as a redundancy matter rather than a capability or conduct issue.*

50. If an employee's work does not reach or falls below the required standard, the following procedure should normally be observed:-

o   the inadequacy should be brought to the employee's attention, an explanation sought and the employee reminded that he or she has a responsibility to achieve the required standard

o   where the reason is because of lack of knowledge of the required standard, the deficiency should be remedied and no disciplinary action taken

o   where the reason is because of illness, accident or advancing age and the employee has a previous good record of competence, the availability of alternative work should be considered

o   where the employee is capable of improvement he or she should be reminded of the standard required and given a reasonable period in which to attain it

o   where the employee has recently been promoted and is having difficulty in coping with the duties at the higher level, he or she should be assisted and encouraged through training or other means to reach an acceptable level of performance

o   the employee should be warned of the likely consequences of future poor work

----

* Redundancy is defined in S81 of the Employment Protection (Consolidation) Act 1978

°   disciplinary action should only be taken if it is clear that the
    fault lies with the employee

°   where the employee is unable to reach the required standard and
    alternative work is not available, the position should be explained
    to the employee before dismissal action is taken.

Action in Particular Cases

51. Employers may wish to consider, in consultation with trade union
officials where appropriate, the introduction of a policy designed to assist
employees who are suffering from alcohol or drug abuse. The aim should be to
identify such employees and motivate them to seek help and treatment and to
help workmates to recognise any problems at an early stage. Factors likely to
constitute early warning signs include absenteeism, poor performance, changes
in personality, irritability, slurred speech, impaired concentration and
memory, deterioration in personal hygiene, anxiety and depression. The policy
should apply to all employees regardless of status or seniority. Where it is
established that an employee is suffering from alcohol or drug abuse,
consideration should be given to whether it is appropriate to treat the
problem as a medical rather than a disciplinary matter. In all cases the
employee should be consulted and encouraged to seek appropriate medical
assistance.

Action in Serious Cases

52. Where the inadequacy of an employee's performance is so extreme or where
the actual or potential consequences of single errors are of an extremely
serious nature, warnings will not normally be appropriate. The disciplinary
procedure should indicate that dismissal action will be taken in such cases.

53. Apart from these exceptional circumstances, an employee should not be
dismissed because of sub-standard work unless warnings have been given.
During the time that warnings are in operation the employee should be given
help and encouragement to enable the required standard to be reached.

PART FIVE: PROCEDURES FOR AVOIDING OR HANDLING REDUNDANCIES

54. This section of the Code aims to give practical guidance to employers and
trade unions on means of avoiding or minimising the effects of redundancies
and lays down guidelines so that decisions about redundancy, where this is
unavoidable, may be made in a consistent and fair manner. Some of the

guidance may not be applicable in the case of small firms where there are constraints of size and administrative resources. The section does not deal with statutory provisions about redundancy notification and consultation on which the Department of Employment issues separate guidance.[*]

Avoiding Redundancies - Planning Ahead

55. Responsibility for deciding the size of the work force rests with management. At the same time management should aim to provide maximum job security for employees by effective manpower planning and, in consultation as appropriate with trade union officials or employee representatives, seek to avoid redundancies wherever possible. Where a labour surplus is expected or arises every effort should be made, consistent with operational efficiency, to absorb the surplus without recourse to compulsory redundancy. Possible measures may include restrictions on recruitment, retraining and redeployment to other parts of the organisation, reduction of overtime, introduction of short-time working, retirement of employees beyond normal retirement age and seeking applicants for early retirement or voluntary redundancy.

Handling Redundancies

56. On occasions when redundancies cannot be avoided, employers should wherever practicable consult their employees or, where trade unions are recognised, their trade union officials as early as possible and ensure that no announcement is made before such consultation has taken place. Consultation may cover:-

  o   the type of redundancy envisaged (e.g. short-term surplus, sectional redundancy, complete closure)

  o   the method of selection for redundancy

  o   the amount of notice and payments to be given to redundant employees if these are to exceed statutory requirements

  o   the effect on earnings where down-grading is accepted in preference to redundancy

----- -------------------

[*]   Part IV of the Employment Protection Act 1975 requires employers to consult with representatives of a recognised trade union about proposed redundancies and to notify the Secretary of State for Employment about certain proposed redundancies.

o   arrangements for travel and for removal expenses where work is accepted in a different location

o   the policy (with particular reference to entitlement to a statutory redundancy payment) should a redundant employee leave during the notice period

o   detailed arrangements for time-off with pay to seek alternative work or to make arrangements for training

o   the terms on which a redundant employee may be re-engaged

o   special arrangements for apprentices.

Redundancy Procedures

57. Management should consider the advantages to be gained by establishing a procedure to be adopted in a redundancy. The initiative for establishing a procedure will normally lie with management but, where appropriate, management should consider whether they should aim to secure the involvement of trade union officials in agreeing the arrangements which will apply to their members. The procedure should be drawn up, if possible, at a time when redundancies are not thought to be imminent and should be made known to all the workforce. The procedure should be regarded as a contingency measure and should be seen simply as one area of personnel work in which it may be prudent to obtain agreement. It should be noted that a management statement of intent or policy on redundancy does not amount to an agreed procedure.

58. Any modification to the procedure either by agreement or by the confirmation of past practice should be incorporated in the procedure and made known to all the workforce. Agreement should be sought before there is any departure from the agreed procedure and, where possible, the procedure should specify the circumstances in which departure may be considered necessary. Where provision is made for the procedure to be applied flexibly to take account of changing economic circumstances, this should also be specified.

Selection Criteria

59. Objective criteria should be applied when determining which employees are to be selected for redundancy and should be agreed where appropriate in consultation with trade union officials. The criteria may include skill, age, length of service, standard of performance including attendance record and

type and mix of employee required in future.   Where the list of agreed criteria is not exhaustive, this should be stated. If attendance records are used as a basis for redundancy selection care should be taken to ensure they are accurate.   It will be helpful if such records show both the extent of and reasons for absence.   Especial care should be exercised where trade union officials may be selected for redundancy.

60. Where the method of selection is based on a policy of last in first out, management should decide, in consultation with trade union officials where appropriate, whether the policy is to be operated across the organisation as a whole or on a departmental basis and whether provision should be made to take account of individual circumstances.   Where selection is based on length of service in a department and not on total service, special attention should be paid to any potential hardship caused to employees who have recently been transferred into particular departments and who would not be selected for redundancy if the policy of last in first out was operated in relation to service as a whole.

61. It will normally be the length of continuous employment which is used to calculate length of service.   The cumulative period of employment, which will normally exclude breaks in service, should only be used when this method of calculation is clearly stated in the agreement.

62. Management should consider, in consultation with trade union officials where appropriate, the establishment of a redundancy appeals procedure to deal with complaints from employees who feel that selection criteria have been unfairly applied in their case.

ASSISTANCE IN FINDING OTHER WORK

63. Employers should consider whether employees likely to be affected by redundancy can be offered alternative work.   Where alternative employment is available within the employer's own organisation or with an associated company, the employee should be given sufficient details to enable him or her to decide whether to accept or not.   Where alternative employment is not available within the employer's own organisation, management should give every assistance to help employees find alternative work elsewhere.   This may take the form of approaches to the appropriate government agencies such as Jobcentres and the Training Service Division of MSC and to other local employers with a view to canvassing for any vacancies which may be offered to the redundant employees.

64. Employees who are under notice of redundancy and who qualify for a statutory redundancy payment also have a statutory entitlement to reasonable paid time off to look for another job or to arrange training.[*] Where possible, employers should extend such assistance to all employees who are affected by redundancy.

Redundancy Counselling

65. Where administrative resources permit, employers should consider the provision of a redundancy counselling service to give redundant employees information not only about alternative sources of employment and training but also about their entitlement to redundancy pay, pension payments and state benefits. Where practicable, redundant employees should be interviewed as early as possible by a counsellor before redundancies are due to take effect and the support and advice should remain available on a regular basis.

Hardship Committees

66. Redundancy is a traumatic experience for many employees especially for those who have been employed for many years in a relatively stable environment. Some employees will have special difficulties to contend with even though they may have received payments in excess of the statutory minimum. To provide assistance for such cases, employers should consider the establishment of hardship committees to consider problems of undue hardship and, where possible, seek ways of alleviating the situation.

Review of Procedures

67. Procedures should be reviewed regularly to ensure that they are operating fairly and to allow for any modifications to be made in the light of changed circumstances.

----
[*] S31 of the Employment Protection (Consolidation) Act 1978, as amended by the Employment Act 1982, entitles certain employees who are given notice of dismissal because of redundancy to reasonable time off with pay during working hours to look for another job or make arrangements for training for future employment. The time off must be allowed before the expiry of the period of notice.

Table of Cases

Note

The following abbreviations are used:

AC – Law Reports, Appeal Cases
All ER – All England Law Reports
Ch – Law Reports, Chancery
CLR – Commonwealth Law Reports
CLY – Current Law Year Book
Crim. LR – Criminal Law Review
DLR – Dominion Law Reports
EAT – Employment Appeal Tribunal
FSR – Fleet Street Law Reports
ICR – Industrial Cases Reports
IRLIB – Industrial Relations Legal Information Bulletin
IRLR – Industrial Relations Law Reports

ITR – Industrial Tribunal Reports
KIR – Knight's Industrial Reports
LGR – Local Government Reports
LJ – Law Journal
NIRC – National Industrial Relations Court
NZLR – New Zealand Law Reports
QBD – Law Reports, Queen's Bench Division
TLR – Times Law Reports
WLR – Weekly Law Reports

References are to section numbers.

Table of Statutes

Statutory Instrument

Index